S
C000183612

Revolutionary Lives

Series Editors: Brian Doherty, Keele University; Sarah Irving, University of Edinburgh; Professor Paul Le Blanc, La Roche College, Pittsburgh

Revolutionary Lives is a series of short, critical biographies of radical figures from throughout history. The books are sympathetic but not sycophantic, and the intention is to present a balanced and, where necessary, critical evaluation of the individual's place in their political field, putting their actions and achievements in context and exploring issues raised by their lives, such as the use or rejection of violence, nationalism, or gender in political activism. While individuals are the subject of the books, their personal lives are dealt with lightly except insofar as they mesh with political concerns. The focus is on the contribution these revolutionaries made to history, an examination of how far they achieved their aims in improving the lives of the oppressed and exploited, and how they can continue to be an inspiration for many today.

Also available:

Salvador Allende:
Revolutionary Democrat
Victor Figueroa Clark

Leila Khaled:
Icon of Palestinian Liberation
Sarah Irving

Jean Paul Marat:
Tribune of the French Revolution
Clifford D. Conner

Gerrard Winstanley:
The Digger's Life and Legacy
John Gurney

www.revolutionarylives.co.uk

Sylvia Pankhurst

Suffragette, Socialist
and Scourge of Empire

Katherine Connelly

PlutoPress
www.plutobooks.com

First published 2013 by Pluto Press
345 Archway Road, London N6 5AA

www.plutobooks.com

Distributed in the United States of America exclusively by
Palgrave Macmillan, a division of St. Martin's Press LLC,
175 Fifth Avenue, New York, NY 10010

British Library Cataloguing in Publication Data
A catalogue record for this book is available from the British Library

ISBN   978 0 7453 3323 6   Hardback
ISBN   978 0 7453 3322 9   Paperback
ISBN   978 1 8496 4942 1   PDF eBook
ISBN   978 1 8496 4944 5   Kindle eBook
ISBN   978 1 8496 4943 8   EPUB eBook

Library of Congress Cataloging in Publication Data applied for

The following photographs are from the Estelle Sylvia Pankhurst collection held at
the International Institute of Social History in Amsterdam: page 13 (in her studio),
page 23 (WSPU's membership card), page 53 (recovering from hunger strike),
page 74 (Cost Price Restaurant) and page 120 (speaking at an anti-Nazi demo).
The photograph on page 107 (in Moscow, at the Third International) is from the
William Gallacher collection, also held at the International Institute of Social
History in Amsterdam.

This book is printed on paper suitable for recycling and made from fully managed
and sustained forest sources. Logging, pulping and manufacturing processes are
expected to conform to the environmental standards of the country of origin.

10   9   8   7   6   5   4   3

Typeset from disk by Stanford DTP Services, Northampton, England
Simultaneously printed in the European Union and the United States of America

Contents

Dedicated with my love
To my parents
Ros and Paul Connelly
Who embody the values celebrated in this book

Acknowledgements

First and foremost I owe a profound debt of gratitude to Sylvia's son, Dr Richard Pankhurst, and to Sylvia's daughter-in-law, Rita Pankhurst. Richard Pankhurst read the manuscript and provided invaluable comments and advice. Throughout the writing of this book they were both always supportive and very generously shared their memories of Sylvia with me. It was a privilege to get to know them and I feel that the interview they gave me greatly enriches this book.

I would also like to thank my publishers Pluto Press for all their help, in particular David Castle who guided me through the entire process and was always supportive and understanding.

I was helped in the commissioning stage by Neil Faulkner, Megan Dobney, Mel Whitter and Des Freedman. I am especially grateful to Tracy Walsh at Ruskin College who gave me one of my first opportunities to present the early ideas for this book and whose kindness and enthusiasm were more than I could ever have hoped or asked for. I would like to thank the students at Ruskin for their thought-provoking contributions which helped me to develop my thoughts. Kate Clayton-Hathway invited me to present my ideas to the Oxford International Women's Festival and I am grateful to her and all those who contributed there. You helped me to pull my last thoughts together.

Explo Nani-Kofi, Leo Zeilig, Marika Sherwood, Hakim Adi, Leslie James and Barbara De Vivo kindly suggested reading material for researching the last chapters of the book. Nigel Shephard generously gave up his time to discuss with me the photographs available in the archives. Jane Mackelworth's research on the suffragettes has opened my eyes to new perspectives and her support has meant a lot to me.

There are many people I would like to thank who are too numerous to mention here and many of whose names I do not know. Firstly, all the people in the social movements that it has been my privilege to campaign alongside in the last ten years. You have educated and inspired me. I would like to thank all the staff at the Tower Hamlets Local History Library, the Working Class Movement Library, the Labour History Archive and Study Centre (People's History Museum/University of Central Lancashire), the Bishopsgate Institute's Library and Archive Collections, the British Library, the Museum of London, the School of Oriental and African Studies' Library, the Marx Memorial Library and especially at the Women's Library where I conducted so much of the research for this book.

I am very grateful to Kings Lynn Trades Council for inviting me to speak at their marvellous 'Women for Change' series and for all the insightful and helpful comments offered by those who attended. In particular I am grateful to their secretary, Jo Rust, who has been very supportive of this book and its subject matter; to William Alderson, who read the manuscript and offered thoughts; and to Jacqueline Mulhallen who read the manuscript, provided me with comments and suggestions, and was extremely generous in her constant support and in sharing her research and ideas on Sylvia in general and her art in particular – I am very much in her debt. Lindsey German, Elaine Graham-Leigh, Lucy Maxwell-Scott, Richard Allday and Ros Connelly also all read the manuscript and provided detailed and extremely useful comments. I am particularly grateful to my mum, Ros Connelly, who also compiled the index and was always on the other end of the phone and always full of encouragement.

This leads me to thanks of a different kind. I am grateful to my friends, and those members of my and Richard's family who were so understanding of my unreliability and sudden absences.

I do not know how to begin to thank my parents Paul and Ros Connelly and my sister Ruth Keogh Connelly for everything they have given me, but I do know that their love, support and understanding while I was writing helped me every single day.

I would like to conclude by thanking my partner Richard Allday who was always willing to share every idea, every development and every setback I faced. His personal commitment to the ideas at the heart of this book, his support, love and comradeship mean the world to me and were a constant source of inspiration while I was writing.

Introduction

The solitary Suffragette who presented herself was able to walk quietly in unnoticed and to take a seat in the middle of the room. If her heart beat so loud that it seemed that all must hear it, if she felt sick and faint with suspense, no one knew.[1]

In the midst of the vast Liberal Party rally just before the 1906 general election, the suffragette waited to ask her question, steeling herself for the violent ejection that invariably followed. The speaker was Winston Churchill, well-known for his particularly 'insulting attitude' towards women's suffrage. When the suffragette stood up and asked her question, 'Will the Liberal Government give women the vote?', he just ignored her. The 'votes for women' banner in her hand was snatched from her, but when some of the men in the audience demanded an answer the chairman invited the suffragette to ask her question from the platform. After doing so, Churchill took her roughly by the arm and forced her into a seat on the platform saying, 'No, you must wait here till you have heard what I have to say', and told the audience 'Nothing would induce me to vote for giving women the franchise.' Suddenly all the men on the platform stood up, blocking the suffragette from view, while others pushed her into a back room.[2] One man went to find a key to lock her in, while another, standing against the door, 'began to use the most violent language and, calling her a cat, gesticulated as though he would scratch her face with his hands'.[3] She ran to the barred window and called out to the people in the street. The threatening man left and the crowd pointed out a window with some bars missing which the suffragette climbed through and then, at the crowd's request, delivered an impromptu speech of her own.

Forty-two years later, and 20 years after all women in Britain won the right to vote, Winston Churchill was still in the House of Commons. On the road outside was a 62-year-old woman in a group holding placards demanding an end to British colonialism in Africa.

In both instances the woman was Sylvia Pankhurst. But what, other than the woman involved, connected the militant suffragette movement to the struggle against colonialism after the Second World War? Sometimes biography enables us to see an alternative political history that upsets the dominant narrative about how political change is achieved.

Standard syllabuses of British political history tend to portray an ascending trajectory of political reform – the reforms drawn up on the Parliamentary benches – punctuated briefly by a few, seemingly unlinked, protests. The story of Sylvia Pankhurst's life – the story from the perspective of the protester locked out of the political meeting and demonstrating on the streets – shows this was never the case. She was a leading suffragette who broke away from the elitism of the suffragette campaign organised by her mother and sister by building a women's suffrage campaign that put working-class women at the forefront of fighting for the vote. In the First World War she campaigned against the intensified exploitation and suffering it brought to working people. She was among the first socialists to champion the Bolshevik revolution, inspired by the soviets which placed direct democracy in the hands of ordinary people. In the 1920s she was one of the first people in Britain to identify the danger posed by the rise of fascism in Italy to democratic freedoms and to peace. At a time when Churchill was proclaiming his admiration for Mussolini she was campaigning against British appeasement of fascism. Her uncompromising opposition to fascism enabled her to be in the forefront of raising awareness about the horror of the Italian invasion of Ethiopia in 1935; a campaign that led her into resisting British attempts to colonise Ethiopia and other parts of Africa after the war.

Despite her lifelong political activism it is for her work as a suffragette, over a period of only ten years of her life, that she is best known. Her role has been written out of not only the dominant historical narratives of twentieth-century politics, but also many studies of the left. In part, this is because after 1921 she was not affiliated to any organisation and so has been difficult to 'claim' as part of a tradition. Many studies of British anti-fascism fail to even mention her unique contribution to this struggle.

Sylvia was above all profoundly committed to a radical, far-reaching conception of democracy for women, for workers and for people struggling to overthrow the dominance of Empire. Her experience of this struggle was that change had to be forced on the privileged classes at Westminster and the gains had to be constantly defended. For those in today's social movements who want to change the world, Sylvia's ideas, campaigns and the dilemmas she was confronted with are more important than we have been led to believe.

1

Portrait of the Artist as a Young Woman

THE PANKHURSTS

I was a child of the late nineteenth century, an inheritor of the struggle for political democracy, not fully accomplished then even for men, whilst women were still outside the political system, profiting by the gains of democracy only adventitiously. The Labour movement for the economic betterment of the masses was stirring towards its birth. The idea of internationalism, in the sense that the world is every man's country, to be valued and respected equally with his birthplace, was gaining ground.[1]

These words, written by Sylvia Pankhurst in 1938, describe the struggles which informed her whole life: the struggles for democracy, women's rights, working-class emancipation, internationalism, and against imperialism.

She was born into a political family at a time of intense political turmoil. Her parents, Emmeline Goulden and Dr Richard Marsden Pankhurst, both came from big Liberal families in Manchester, the city of manufacture and commerce that epitomised nineteenth-century Liberalism. Emmeline Goulden was the eldest daughter of Robert Goulden, a partner in a cotton printing and bleaching firm and local Liberal councillor. Richard Pankhurst, the son of a Liberal Baptist Dissenter, worked as a barrister. In the late 1870s the Conservative government allied itself with the repressive Turkish Empire, almost dragging Britain into war with Russia, and fought unpopular and disastrous wars in Afghanistan and South Africa. Emmeline and Richard met in the ferment of the antiwar agitation championed by the Liberal Party, and married in 1879. They shared a passion for radical politics and challenging injustice; in their short courtship Richard wrote to Emmeline 'every struggling cause shall be ours'.[2]

Only 21 when she married, Emmeline had attended her first women's suffrage meeting at the age of 14. Richard, who was 20 years older, had been involved in politics for far longer. He declared himself a republican in the 1870s, campaigned for the abolition of the House of Lords, was a prominent supporter of women's suffrage and Home Rule for Ireland, and championed the Mechanics Institutes, which pioneered working-class higher education.

In 1880 their first child, Christabel Harriette, was born, and became, by all accounts, her mother's favourite child. On the 5th of May 1882 their second child Estelle Sylvia was born. The name Estelle, which had been chosen by her mother, was swiftly rejected by the independent-minded child who insisted on using her middle name which had been chosen by her father, something that perhaps strengthened the very close relationship she had with him. Three more children followed: Henry Francis Robert (Frank) was born in 1884, but died in 1888, Adela Constantia Mary was born in 1885, and Henry Francis (Harry) in 1889.

A year after Sylvia's birth, Richard Pankhurst declared his intention to run in a Manchester by-election, publicly backed by his father-in-law Robert Goulden whose home the Pankhursts had moved into. However, since the Liberal Party had come into office in 1880 all the idealism it expressed in opposition had melted away. Richard resigned from the local Liberal Association and ran as an independent candidate, openly criticising the Liberal government's repressive policies in India and Ireland.[3] He was to pay a high price for his radical programme. Even though the only other candidate in the election was a Conservative, the Liberal Association called on its members not to vote for Richard Pankhurst and the Liberal press attacked him as a 'wild extremist'.[4] Richard lost the election and his rebellious stance saw him subject to a professional boycott. His reaction to this would generate profound political and personal changes for the Pankhurst family.

ALL THAT IS SOLID MELTS INTO AIR:
THE POLITICS OF THE 1880s

Immediately after the 1883 election Richard helped found a
Radical Association to challenge the Liberals and took up the
case of a fruit and vegetable salesman against the powerful
Corporation of Manchester.[5] This was all rather too much for the
respectable businessman Robert Goulden to tolerate, especially
as he found his own business was now being boycotted. After a
series of bitter arguments the Pankhursts left the Goulden home
and moved to London. Emmeline never spoke to her father
again. It was instilled into Sylvia from an early age that principles
came first no matter what the financial or personal cost.

The Pankhursts' political trajectory reflected the wider social
and political developments of the 1880s. The antiwar movement
of the late 1870s had radicalised many of its supporters who,
like Richard Pankhurst, became disillusioned with the Liberal
government and began to look for new ideas which resonated
with their desire for radical social change. New radical and
socialist organisations sprang up: the Democratic Federation,
established in 1881, became the more socialist Social Democratic
Federation in 1884, and in the same year the Fabian Society
and the Socialist League were formed. In 1886 a demonstration
protesting at the destitution faced by the unemployed turned
violent and leading socialists were put on trial. A year later a
demonstration in Trafalgar Square against repression in Ireland
was met by mounted police who attacked the protestors on what
became known as 'Bloody Sunday'. In response, campaigns for
free speech were launched. In 1888 hundreds of matchwomen
in East London went on strike, marched on Parliament, formed
a union and won their dispute. Their action inspired other
groups of workers, who were classed as 'unskilled' and left
unorganised by the trade unions, to take militant strike action
and form their own unions. A year after the matchwomen,
the gas workers struck, swiftly followed by the Great Dock
Strike which galvanised hundreds of thousands of workers
into activity and a wave of strike action across the country.
This was described as New Unionism and it was evident why:

in 1889 union membership had stood at 860,000
stood at nearly 2 million.[6] New Unionism marked
working-class militancy and self-organisation that had not been
seen since the Chartist movement in the 1840s. In ten years the
landscape of stale political certainties had been transformed into
one characterised by strikes, protests and acute social tensions.

In 1885 Richard Pankhurst again stood unsuccessfully
for Parliament, but this time as a Radical for the London
constituency of Rotherhithe. In the mid 1880s Richard and
Emmeline continued their political trajectory away from their
Liberal Party backgrounds, joining the moderate socialist Fabian
Society and participating in the free speech agitation. But like
many of the moderate socialists they had only marginal contact
with New Unionism – apart from mixing with some of the labour
movement leaders and donating money to the matchwomen's
strike fund, they kept their distance from the huge strike wave.

EMANCIPATION BEGINS AT HOME

Whereas many suffragette memoirs tell of childhood battles for
the right, as daughters, to spend time reading, Sylvia Pankhurst
recalled of her London childhood: 'we chose what books we
pleased at the London Library, and any in the house; there
were no barriers'.[7] The enlightened Dr Pankhurst encouraged
his daughters to read voraciously: 'For many years he brought
a book home to us every night; history, travel, simple science,
astronomy, botany, chemistry, engineering, fairy-tales, standard
novels, reproductions of works of art, the best illustrations.'[8]
He read them the radical poetry of Shelley and Whitman, and
Sylvia's writings about her early life are filled with the vivid
impressions from her childhood reading.[9] Imaginative and
emotional, Sylvia was haunted by the depictions of poverty in
Dickens's novels: 'they dealt me horrible dreams and sleepless
nights; but they made real for me the cause of the People and
the Poor. The miseries of Oliver Twist and the other exploited
children bit deep into my little heart.'[10]

Defying the social expectation that young middle-class women should concentrate on getting married and confining themselves to the home, Sylvia recalled that her father impressed upon his daughters the importance of working for a living: 'When we were still but toddlers he was for ever asking us: "What do you want to be when you grow up?" and urging: "Get something to earn your living by that you like and can do."'[11]

Sylvia's vocation, from very early childhood, was art, and this was encouraged despite the precarity of an artistic profession. She was deeply influenced by the art produced by Walter Crane for the labour movement, such as his drawings celebrating May Day, and by William Morris's evocations of egalitarian societies – in particular she was struck by Morris's illustration accompanying the lines 'When Adam delved and Eve span, who was then the gentleman', in his *A Dream of John Ball* (1888).[12] Her earliest ideas about art were thus inextricably linked with the struggle for a better world, and one of her earliest ambitions was to make that struggle itself beautiful, aesthetically uplifting and inspiring:

> I would be a decorative painter; I would portray the world that is to be when poverty is no more. I would decorate halls where people would foregather in the movement to win the new world, and make banners for the meetings and processions. I had been with my parents to meetings of the social [sic] Democratic Federation in dingy rooms in back streets, and to drab and dreary demonstrations in Hyde Park; I wanted to make these beautiful.[13]

The Pankhursts' unusual childhood was compounded by the fact that their mother refused to allow them to go to school while they lived in London, declaring that 'I want to develop their individuality above all things.'[14] They were therefore erratically educated by a series of governesses and derived an extensive political awareness at the meetings their parents held, attended by figures from across the contemporary radical movements: 'The house was soon a centre for many gatherings, of Socialists, Fabians, Anarchists, Suffragists, Free Thinkers, Radicals and Humanitarians of all schools.'[15]

'IMMEDIATE AND UNCONDITIONAL EMANCIPATION': THE LESSONS OF THE WOMEN'S FRANCHISE LEAGUE

In the late nineteenth century the argument over how radical the women's suffrage movement should be centred around the problem of 'coverture' – the status imposed on wives under English common law which denied them a legal existence independent of their husband. In the 1860s the parliamentary Bills for women's suffrage made no mention of coverture, and many of the campaigners for these Bills were working to dismantle coverture. Richard Pankhurst drafted the Married Women's Property Act, giving married women the right to their own property, which was passed into law in 1882, the year Sylvia was born. It seemed that by the time women's suffrage was granted coverture would be abolished and so all women, whether married or not, would win the vote. However, from 1874, after the Liberal Jacob Bright lost his seat and the women's suffrage movement their most radical supporter in Parliament, MPs began to introduce women's suffrage Bills which explicitly *excluded* married women, a development that was tolerated by the women's suffrage societies. But by 1889, when Liberal MP William Woodall introduced a Bill with the proviso 'that nothing in this Act contained shall enable women under coverture to be registered to vote at such elections', the social and political tempo outside Parliament had changed.[16] A group of campaigners, mostly Radical Liberals, feminists who were openly critical of marriage, and some members of the new socialist organisations, organised to fight this discriminatory clause and in 1889 split from the other suffrage societies to form the Women's Franchise League (WFL).

The Pankhursts were leading members of the WFL which, from the start, made it clear that they rejected the idea that the fight for women's suffrage could be separated from the wider struggle for women's emancipation. The WFL inaugural meeting was addressed by William Lloyd Garrison whose father, of the same name, had been prominent in the American struggle to abolish slavery. Lloyd Garrison likened the suffrage movement to the anti-slavery movement. He asserted that the approach of the 'moderates' was worse than the 'openly frank and brutal' opposition of the slave-holders, for they 'were always trying to temper zeal, weaken testimony, decry strong language, and apologise for the wrong-doer'. Meanwhile, the Abolitionists' 'only response was "immediate and unconditional emancipation." They knew full well that the moral force of their uncompromising advocacy would mould legislation more powerfully than temporising and wire-pulling to accomplish partial Acts.'[17]

Richard Pankhurst endorsed this message: 'We will not take a piece of justice if thereby we prejudice and injure all the rest.'[18] In 1890 the WFL called an International Conference held at the Pankhursts' home in London which proclaimed the 'modern movement' to be one that 'seeks to place society in all its relations upon principles of equal justice, [and] has necessarily attacked the privileges and disabilities grounded on colour, race, religion, and class'.[19]

The WFL lasted only into the early 1890s, disintegrating shortly after the Pankhursts moved back to Manchester, but it was the radical tradition of social struggle that it represented, its insistence on going on the offensive in campaigns and refusing to submit to divisions encouraged from above, that inspired the early militant suffragettes and Sylvia's lifelong vision of campaigning.

SYLVIA'S FIRST CAMPAIGNS

By the beginning of the 1890s New Unionism found itself faced with a huge bosses' offensive. The strike wave that had seen such significant victories was now experiencing devastating defeats; some employers imposed a lock-out on workers, starving them into submission. Some socialists began to argue that resorting to offensive strike action had been wrong all along, and that instead workers should focus their efforts on achieving reforms through Parliament. At the beginning of the 1890s thousands of workers striking against wage cuts in Bradford's Manningham Mills were starved back to work, and it was in Bradford, symbolically, that the Independent Labour Party (ILP) was founded in January 1893.[20] The turn towards a political route was not seen as a way of strengthening a working-class movement which could challenge capitalism but was designed to substitute for such a movement, maintaining that an equal and just society could be created through parliamentary reforms alone. This was the view of socialism that Richard and Emmeline Pankhurst were comfortable with. Unlike revolutionary socialists such as Eleanor Marx, who was deeply involved in New Unionism, helping in the day-to-day running of the strikes and discussing political strategies, the Pankhursts were not in favour of spreading industrial action. Indeed at the 1898 ILP Conference Richard Pankhurst moved the resolution reading: 'That this conference of Socialists deplores the action of trades unionists in resorting to strikes to obtain industrial reform, and declares in favour of political action for labour reform.'[21] He then went on to add that 'the serious questions which were usually involved in strikes should be left to the responsible settlement of Parliament'.[22] The Pankhursts were more comfortable viewing workers as victims whom they could speak *on behalf of*. They were thus predisposed to the ILP, becoming early leading members of the organisation, and forming a close friendship with Keir Hardie, one of the ILP's founding members.

But Sylvia did not experience this change in orientation in the same way her parents did. As a young child in London she had been largely confined to the home, meeting only figureheads from the labour movement. As a teenager in Manchester she was able to go out campaigning alongside her parents in the new socialist campaigns. From Sylvia's perspective, the 1890s marked not a retreat from class struggle to more politically focused action, but a move towards the working class as she was now meeting working-class people in significant numbers for the first time. She helped her mother distribute food to the destitute unemployed in the winter of 1894–5, finding herself 'heartsick at the grim sight of those hungry thousands waiting in the bitter cold to receive that meagre aid'.[23] She went with her father when he spoke to crowds in the working-class districts of Manchester, and when Richard stood as the ILP candidate

for Gorton in 1895 (again he was unsuccessful) she went out
canvassing for him and heard the terrible experiences of poor
families.[24] Above all, these experiences filled her with a profound
anger against poverty:

> I would ask myself whether it could be just that I should live in Victoria
> Park,* and go well fed and warmly clad, whilst the children of these grey
> slums were lacking the very necessities of life. The misery of the poor, as
> I heard my father plead for it, and saw it revealed in the pinched faces of
> his audiences, awoke in me a maddening sense of impotence; and there
> were moments when I had the impulse to dash my head against the dreary
> walls of those squalid streets.[25]

Now allowed to attend school, she expressed her growing socialist
ideas there only to find herself ridiculed by fellow pupils as well
as the staff: 'In reply to one of my essays in the composition
class even one of the teachers had asked me: "If there were no
poverty, what would become of all our charities?"'[26]

In 1896 Sylvia participated in the campaign against the decision
by the City Council Park Committee to ban mass meetings held
by the ILP in Manchester's open-air Boggart Hole Clough. The
ILP raised the stakes when Emmeline Pankhurst began to address
the meetings. She was a prominent local figure having been
recently elected top of the poll as an ILP candidate to the Board
of Guardians, the body that administered provisions for the
poor. She declared that she would pay no fine for committing
the offence, daring the courts to imprison her. As *The Labour
Leader* newspaper noted, she was not the only family member
to take part in the acts of civil disobedience in the Clough, as
'Dr. Pankhurst's two charming girls, Christobel [*sic*] and Sylvia,
have been collecting [money at the meetings] each Sunday, but
the Parks Committee have not yet got their courage up to the
point of summoning them.'[27]

As the Parks Committee proved less determined than the
Pankhursts, and the courts continually adjourned the case against

---

* The Pankhursts lived in Victoria Park, a middle-class part of Manchester.

Emmeline, reluctant to imprison a prominent middle-class woman, the ban was overturned. The Boggart Hole Clough agitation had shown that determination to break the law could change the law – a valuable lesson for the Pankhursts in their future struggles.

ART AND CONFLICT

In 1898 Sylvia was left devastated when her father, the person to whom she was closer than anyone else, died suddenly. Adding to her pain was the fact that her mother and older sister were abroad and Sylvia, aged 16 and left in charge, was filled with intense self-reproach for not having called her mother home sooner.[28] Left with no income they had to move to a smaller house and sell their possessions, for which purpose they invited Richard Pankhurst's friend and admirer of the Pre-Raphaelites, Charles Rowley, to advise on the value of their paintings. Sylvia remembered that Rowley was more struck by her own drawings

Sylvia Pankhurst the art student in her studio, c. 1904.

'and said I was more promising than the pictures'.[29] They sent Sylvia's work to the Municipal School of Art which won her a free studentship there. Although relishing the chance to develop as an artist she soon found herself confronted with political dilemmas. After the coronation of Edward VII in 1901, Sylvia, along with other art students, was commissioned to illustrate a page in an illuminated address to greet the King on his visit to Manchester. The profoundly republican Sylvia fulfilled the commission before going among the welcoming crowds to sell Keir Hardie's pamphlet on unemployment titled 'Open Letter to the King'.[30]

In 1899 Britain plunged into another war, this time the Boer War in South Africa. The government and the press helped to whip up a tide of patriotic fervour which even some left-wing organisations were unable to resist. In 1900 Emmeline Pankhurst left the Fabian Society in protest at their refusal to oppose the war. At this time Sylvia attended a lecture given by Walter Crane at the School of Art during which he drew Britannia's trident and made the critical comment 'Let her be as careful to respect the liberties of others as she is in safeguarding her own', which Sylvia reported for the school's magazine. Another student who demonstrated her patriotism by dressing in khaki, demanded the removal of the article 'declaring that she would follow me home and break our windows'.[31] The Pankhurst family suffered considerable victimisation during the Boer War. Adela and Harry, who were both still at school, made their antiwar views known, for which Harry was beaten unconscious and Adela was hit in the face by a book thrown by another student, an action that was left unreproached by the teacher.[32]

In 1902 Sylvia's exceptional artistic talents were recognised when she was awarded a number of prizes including the Proctor Travelling Studentship, the highest prize awarded by the School of Art, which enabled her to study abroad. Sylvia chose Venice where she spent months copying the city's dazzling mosaics as well as going into the streets to paint the ordinary Venetians – a precursor to her later studies of working people. She also flouted convention by asking to be admitted to the Academia delle Belle Arti's life-drawing class where there were no women students. Although directed to work alone in the antique room, Sylvia was not so easily disarmed: 'I guessed that I should never get into the life class if I waited to be sent there, and next day I simply walked in.'[33]

From then on she took the class alongside the male students.

After her return to Britain in the spring of 1903 Sylvia was to experience far worse discrimination at the hands of the British artistic establishment. She came top of the list of those who entered for a National Scholarship to study at the Royal College of Art in London in 1904 but soon found that however talented the women students were they were not treated as equals by the College. In fact discrimination against women was institutionalised:

> The attitude of the all-male staff of the college was chauvinistic and patronising. They assumed that all women students would automatically become teachers, and not professional artists. Since most graduates, male or female, tended to earn their living initially by teaching, women graduates could only take up the posts still available after all the male graduates had taken their pick.
>
> Although there were three hundred students, the accommodation they occupied (above part of the V&A) was very restricted. At some classes, such as life drawing, the men were allowed to take their places first, and only as many women students as could be fitted in would make up the class.[34]

On arrival Sylvia was 'informed by the students that there was great discrimination against women students in the award of prizes and scholarships obtainable at the college'. Sylvia had already become something of a spokesperson for the students, going to the Principal to inform him of the widespread resentment over the extensive and compulsory focus on architecture. Rebellious women students were not taken kindly to and she was 'ordered furiously from the room. Thereafter, whenever I met the Principal in the corridor, we glared at each other, like two savage dogs.'[35]

Not one to let this deter her from taking up the issue of the scholarships, Sylvia had her old family friend Keir Hardie raise this as a question in Parliament. The answer that scholarships were awarded on a ratio of one woman to 13 men confirmed the long suspected discrimination. Despite her confidence in speaking up, Sylvia was personally very shy and she seems to have made only one real friend at the College, Amy Browning, a fellow rebellious student who had her own conflicts with the management. But by this time the shy and distant art student was living a double life – outside college she was helping to lead a new, militant protest movement.

2
Suffragettes, Socialism and Sacrifice

In the early 1900s the Pankhursts were swept up in the project to achieve independent working-class representation in Parliament. In 1900 the Trades Union Congress (TUC) initiated a conference, attended in the majority by trade unionists but also supported by socialist groups including the ILP, to form the Labour Representation Committee (LRC), which by 1906 had become the Labour Party. In the 1900 general election two LRC candidates were elected to Parliament, one of whom was the Pankhurst family's friend Keir Hardie.

These developments had far-reaching implications for the women's suffrage movement. The activists in this movement, known as 'suffragists', had traditionally been allied with the Liberal Party. In 1897 the women's suffrage organisations united to form the National Union of Women's Suffrage Societies (NUWSS) under the presidency of Liberal stalwart Millicent Garrett Fawcett. The influence of the new idea of working-class representation was most clearly seen in the Northwest where women in the cotton industry were the most densely unionised of all groups of women workers. In the summer of 1903 they formed 'the first organization of working women for the vote', the Lancashire and Cheshire Women Textile and Other Workers' Representation Committee.[1] In their ground-breaking study of these activists, historians Liddington and Norris dubbed these campaigners the 'radical suffragists'. However, although the radical suffragists identified their struggle for women's rights with the labour struggle, not all sections of the labour movement were committed to challenging oppression. Since only men who occupied property worth at least £10 a year were entitled to vote – which excluded around 40 per cent of the poorest men – votes for women 'on the same terms as men' would also see a large proportion of poor women excluded from the vote. Some opponents of women's suffrage seized on this to denounce the women's suffrage campaign as not sufficiently democratic, claiming instead to support adult suffrage – votes for all. At the 1901 TUC Conference a women's suffrage resolution introduced by the President of the Wigan Weavers Union was defeated by a rival resolution for adult suffrage. The women's suffrage advocates argued that the question was simply one of opposing discrimination and were furious that leading figures from across the labour movement, who were doing nothing to campaign for adult suffrage, were using it merely as a device to stifle the women's movement. In August 1903 Christabel Pankhurst, who had developed an interest in women's suffrage, complained that the relationship between the women's and labour movements was one-sided: 'The L.R.C. invites the support of women's unions – what has it to offer in return if it does not intend to press for the representation of women's labour?'[2]

While these tensions mounted over the summer of 1903, Sylvia was absorbed with her most important artistic commission to date: the decoration of Pankhurst Hall, built in memory of her father. She accomplished the task in less than three months, covering the walls in images of the natural world accompanied by lines of poetry from Richard's beloved Shelley. It was as if her childhood dream, to decorate halls for the people, to beautify the struggle for socialism, had come true; even her childhood inspiration Walter Crane came to speak at the opening. However, there was an unpleasant shock awaiting the Pankhursts. The hall dedicated to Richard Pankhurst, a constant ally in the struggle for women's rights, was to be used by an ILP branch that did not allow women to join. This betrayal, Sylvia later wrote, 'proved the last straw which caused Mrs Pankhurst to decide on the formation of a new organization of women'.[3] On the 10th of October 1903 Emmeline invited local ILP women to her house where they formed the Women's Social and Political Union (WSPU) to campaign for votes for women.

EARLY WORKING-CLASS MILITANCY

Despite its tensions with sections of the labour movement, the WSPU was firmly rooted within it and, like the radical suffragists, represented another break from the women's suffrage movement's historic allegiance to the Liberals. The early WSPU consisted of local ILP members who found their primary audience in the labour movement. Teresa Billington (later Billington-Greig), a teacher in Manchester, ILP member, and one of the earliest WSPU members, would later recall:

> all doors in the progressive movements were open to us in our campaign for an equal suffrage bill. We won a hearing in them from Fabian groups and Labour Churches to trade union branch meetings and odd groups meeting in odd corners such as basements and barns where they devised the making of a new world.[4]

Annie Kenney, a cotton mill worker who became one of the most famous WSPU members, joined at an Oldham Trades Council meeting addressed by Teresa Billington and Christabel Pankhurst.[5] The early WSPU members were actively involved with other progressive campaigns, for example Teresa Billington helped form the Manchester Equal Pay League.[6] These wider links informed their understanding of the kind of changes they wanted the vote to bring about, thus Annie Kenney later wrote about speaking in Manchester's Tib Street (itself a favourite meeting place for the local labour movement): 'I supposed I touched on Labour, the unemployed, children and finally summed up the whole thing by saying something about Votes for Women.'[7]

In drawing on the support of the labour movement as well as its traditions of street meetings, the early WSPU closely resembled the radical suffragists. However, unlike the radial suffragists, who confined their activity to the Northwest, the WSPU set its sights on building a national organisation. The tactics it employed to propel its small organisation to national attention were themselves inspired by contemporary social movements.

In 1905 a campaign demanding the government provide work for the unemployed attracted a high profile when a thousand poor women from London's East End marched on Parliament, while in Manchester four men on an unemployment protest were arrested for blocking a road.[8] The approaching general election, to be held early in 1906, provided the opportunity for the WSPU to use similar direct action tactics to turn women's suffrage into an election issue. As it was generally, and accurately, anticipated that the Conservative government would fall and be replaced by a Liberal government, the WSPU campaigned for a Liberal commitment to women's suffrage. On the 13th of October 1905 Christabel Pankhurst and Annie Kenney went to a large Liberal meeting in Manchester's Free Trade Hall and asked the speaker, Sir Edward Grey, if a Liberal government would grant votes for women. When he ignored the question the women stood on their seats and heckled, demanding an answer, until they were roughly ejected from the meeting and arrested. When asked in court to choose between paying a fine or imprisonment they both chose to go to prison. Christabel was sentenced to seven days, Annie Kenney to three.

These combative campaign tactics, known as militancy, decisively marked the WSPU out from the suffragists, leading to the WSPU being dubbed 'suffragettes' by the press – a title they proudly adopted.

Sylvia, now living in London, was initially more involved with the labour movement than the women's movement. A member of the Fulham ILP branch, she continued to lend her artistic skills to the socialist movement. Her support for the unemployment campaign is evident in the campaign poster she was commissioned to design in which she depicted the unemployed workers not as weak victims but as heroic and muscular figures, both male and female, on the march for their rights.

However, when the suffragettes achieved national notoriety with the 1905 arrests the Pankhursts decided it was time to move the focus to London and escalate the campaign. Christabel, completing her law degree in Manchester, could not immediately move, so Sylvia was persuaded to become the WSPU's first honorary secretary. Committee meetings were held in her student lodgings, and Annie Kenney was sent to help. Emmeline Pethick-Lawrence, the woman the WSPU charmed into becoming their treasurer, was dismayed to find 'there was no office, no organization, no money – no postage stamps even'. She recalled that 23-year-old Sylvia, charged with launching a national campaign while studying and trying to establish herself as an artist, 'looked over-burdened and distraught'.[9]

Sylvia's actions in this leadership role provide a valuable insight into her early interpretation of militancy. From the start, she not only drew inspiration from the tactics of the unemployment agitation, she also sought to involve the women themselves engaged in that campaign. 'It was easy for me to decide that we should follow all the other popular movements by holding a meeting in Trafalgar Square, and a procession of the East London women in the unemployed movement at the opening of Parliament.'[10]

She sent Annie Kenney to the East End of London where, through ILP contacts, she met women activists in the unemployment movement. The early suffragette campaign in London was thus heavily influenced by the traditions of the labour movement. When Sylvia and the small band of WSPU members organised a meeting in Caxton Hall to coincide with the opening of Parliament in February 1906, hundreds of East End women marched there from the station carrying red flags.[11] Indeed, the WSPU's own banner, red with white lettering, looked like a labour banner.[12] Annie Kenney remembered that at Caxton Hall the women 'waved the Red Flag and sang the "Red Flag" so loudly that the strangers present must have thought they had made a mistake and that it was a meeting prepared for Tom Mann'.[*13]

So solidly working class was the WSPU's audience that two upper-class ladies came in disguise in their maids' clothes so as not to stand out.[14]

---

* Tom Mann was one of the leaders of the Dock Strike in 1889, a socialist and ILP member.

Just over a week later, the Unemployed Women of South West Ham voted to become the Canning Town branch of the WSPU. The first London branch of the WSPU met in the ILP Club and encouraged their members to join the ILP.[15] They saw the vote as a means towards huge social changes in working women's lives and this evidently resonated with women locally: throughout 1906–7 they held weekly meetings regularly attended by upwards of 40 women.[16] Annie Kenney recalled one such meeting of 'the very poorest women in Canning Town' where

> Sylvia and I told them all the wonderful things that would happen to them once women got the vote. Poverty would be practically swept away; washing would be done by municipal machinery! In fact Paradise would be there once the Vote was won![17]

A WSPU leaflet produced while Sylvia was honorary secretary presented the vote as a tool for working women which would enable them to increase the parliamentary representation of their class: 'The Vote is the Organised Workers' most powerful weapon as men are now finding out. The Labour Party is the best proof of how the Vote can benefit the workers.'[18]

The extent to which Sylvia envisaged the campaign being led by working-class women is evident in the WSPU membership card she designed around this time. The sole image is a procession of women whose rolled up sleeves, clogs and aprons makes them instantly recognisable as women workers. The style is reminiscent of the poster she designed for the unemployment campaign, in its use of block colours, and the dress and gestures of the figures, which further indicates the link she made between these struggles.[19]

Like the labour and free speech movements before them, the WSPU organised street protests. At a protest outside the house of the new Liberal Prime Minster, Henry Campbell-Bannerman, calling on him to grant the women's suffrage movement an audience, Annie Kenney was arrested alongside two working-class recruits from the East End, Mrs Sparboro and Mrs Knight. In court, all three chose to go to prison for six weeks rather than pay a fine. The protest worked: Campbell-Bannerman agreed

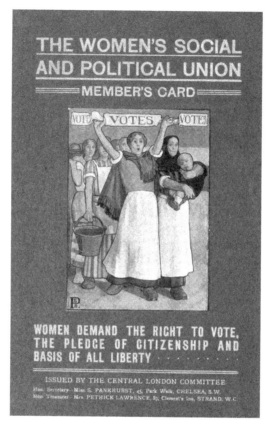

The WSPU's membership card designed by Sylvia (c. 1906–7) shows working-class women at the forefront of the early militant suffragette movement.

to see a deputation of women's suffrage organisations. Working women marched from the East End to attend, and when the Prime Minister gave no guarantee that the government would introduce a women's suffrage bill, Annie Kenney 'jumped on a chair and shouted: "Sir, we are not satisfied! The agitation will go on!"'[20] They then marched to Trafalgar Square and held 'the first great open air public meeting for Women's Suffrage ever held in London'.[21]

The links the first suffragettes had with the labour movement significantly helped to expand their organisation. The first WSPU organisers were experienced campaigners, used to recruiting members to socialist organisations.[22] Keir Hardie, now leader of the Labour Party, helped raise hundreds of pounds which enabled the small organisation to hire big London halls, ensuring large audiences could hear the charismatic leaders speak and recruit members.[23] Hardie also introduced the WSPU to Frederick and Emmeline Pethick-Lawrence. Well-connected, well-off and owning a flat and offices, from which Frederick Pethick-Lawrence ran the socialist publication *The Labour Record*, they were very much the kind of people the WSPU wanted to meet. When both agreed to become involved in the WSPU they provided the suffragettes with office space, publicity in *The Labour Record*, and, in Emmeline Pethick-Lawrence, a remarkable talent for fundraising. All this, combined with imaginative, audacious stunts drawn from the direct actions of the new street movements rather than the traditions of the old parliamentary parties, won members to the WSPU across the country.

Sylvia therefore presided over a campaign which organised primarily amongst working-class women in the East End, used militancy to obtain practical gains such as audiences with ministers, and worked closely with the labour movement and campaigns the East End women were involved in. She presented the vote as an integral part of obtaining the social changes these women were already engaged in fighting for. In all these ways, the early WSPU closely resembled the suffrage organisation Sylvia was later to build from 1912.

TENSIONS WITH LABOUR

Sylvia's leadership role was short-lived. Emmeline insisted that Sylvia should remain honorary secretary until Christabel could come to London to control the hand-over of the post, but Sylvia refused to cooperate. She left her student lodgings shortly before a WSPU committee meeting was due to take place there, leaving her resignation letter on the table thereby forcing the London committee to choose their own leaders. They selected two socialist members, Charlotte Despard and Edith How-Martyn, to jointly hold the post. Sylvia's rebellion was partly motivated by the approaching end of her studies and need to find time to try and earn a living, but it also pointed to her opposition to Christabel's political leadership: 'in spite of my love for Christabel, I was, even then, not fully in accord with the spirit of her policy'.[24] Unlike Sylvia, Christabel did not involve herself in any other campaigns for radical social change – she only cared about women's suffrage. Although she oversaw the movement in the Northwest which was closely allied with the labour movement, from Christabel's perspective this was far more from necessity than a sense of common interests. This became more obvious after Christabel took control of the national organisation from late 1906 and rapidly began to break all links with the labour movement. This manifested itself in the changed approach to adult suffrage and a new by-election policy.

Although some supporters of adult suffrage were suspected of holding this position purely out of a hostility to women's rights, others, like the leading women's trade unionist Margaret Bondfield who helped establish the Adult Suffrage Society in 1904, were genuinely committed to it and saw anything less as a betrayal of their class.[25] The early WSPU initially argued that they supported adult suffrage in principle; at the 1905 ILP Conference Teresa Billington acknowledged the limitations of a Bill to grant women's suffrage on the same terms as men but argued that its passing would help the fight for a more democratic electoral system: 'We have been twitted that the Bill is opposed to the adult suffrage movement. It is nothing of the kind. It is a step towards it – a practical, achievable step.'[26]

That the disagreement was initially more about tactics than principles was reflected in the vacillations of Keir Hardie, one of the WSPU's staunchest supporters. In the first year of the WSPU's life he commissioned an ILP survey to determine the proportion of working-class women who would be enfranchised by a Bill granting women the vote on the same terms as men. Although the survey, completed by a minority of ILP branches, was hardly representative, its finding that the vast majority would be working class was used by Hardie to bolster support for women's suffrage.[27] When the 1907 Labour Party Conference voted to support adult suffrage Hardie threatened to resign, while at a WSPU meeting in March he offended that audience by stating that if women's suffrage was not granted within two years, a movement for adult suffrage would emerge.[28] Sylvia later felt that the WSPU were tactically wrong to have nothing positive to say about adult suffrage: 'a grave mistake was made in leaving the field of adult suffrage – the true field of the Labour movement – to those who were either hostile or indifferent to the inclusion of women'.[29]

Perhaps if Sylvia's approach of uniting the women's suffrage campaign with the wider goals of the labour movement had been maintained, the two sides could have worked together more closely in a progressive alliance. Had the supportive relationship that was emerging between the ILP and the WSPU in East London in early 1906 been built on, then suspicions on both sides might have been broken down, isolating the chauvinists hiding behind adult suffrage. However, as the WSPU separated its struggle from the wider battles for democracy, women's suffrage was increasingly presented as an end in itself rather than a tactical stepping stone towards adult suffrage, making any cooperation between the women's and adult suffrage supporters impossible.

Christabel's new by-election policy further strained the suffragettes' relationship with Labour. In response to the Liberal government's refusal to support women's suffrage the WSPU would campaign against the Liberal candidates in by-elections thereby forcing the Liberals to reconsider or risk losing seats in the House of Commons. However, Christabel insisted upon strict neutrality towards the other parties. Labour was angered by the WSPU's refusal to recognise that they were the only party committed to franchise reform, while the WSPU slogan 'Keep the Liberal Out' suggested the suffragettes were calling on the electorate to vote for the party which had the best chance of defeating the Liberals, and in almost every case that was the second most powerful party in Parliament – the Conservatives. At a by-election in Bury St Edmunds in August 1907, Sylvia was dismayed to find this very situation. In this rural town where there was no Labour candidate, the workers supported the Liberal, while the Conservative candidate was a member of the powerful Guinness family. Sylvia felt that the other suffragettes sent to assist the campaign were hardly neutral, being 'instinctively hostile to other classes and other races, and to social reform of any kind'.[30] One local paper, which supported Walter Guinness, was convinced that the suffragettes were calling for a vote for the Conservatives:

> the Suffragettes are carrying on an active campaign and are canvassing on behalf of Mr. Guinness ... They have had experience of how little faith can be put in the promises of Sir Henry Campbell-Bannerman, and will not lift a finger in support of a Radical.[31]

In response to accusations that the WSPU was being paid by the Conservatives, Sylvia told an audience that the Pankhursts were socialists, for which Christabel rebuked her.[32]

Sylvia later questioned the whole policy of intervening in by-elections:

> If the Suffragettes had never intervened in the elections, if they had gone there to oppose all Parties, or no Parties, given the determination of women to go to prison to advance their cause, the movement would have grown and flourished.[33]

She also believed that from 'very early' Christabel 'based her hope and her policy on the speedy return of a Conservative Government'.[34] Sylvia's suspicions were correct. In October 1907 Christabel was privately, and unsuccessfully, urging the Conservative Party leader, Balfour, to state that he would grant women's suffrage if in office on the basis that this 'would prevent the threatened alliance of a large section of the women's suffrage party with the Labour Party'.[35]

DEMOCRACY AND CLASS STRUGGLE

The shift away from socialist organisations coincided with a change in the WSPU's structure. Formed by women familiar with the traditions of labour organisations, the WSPU had, in theory, a democratic constitution where local branches elected delegates to attend an annual conference to vote on its policy and leadership.[36] However, some members, like Teresa Billington, felt that in practice their ideas were marginalized: 'on the question of tactics there was an invisible wall between the ordinary member and the Pankhurst family'. She hoped that the 1907 conference would provide an opportunity to regain democratic control.[37] Sensing a challenge to the leadership, Emmeline Pankhurst literally tore up the constitution. Sylvia, who was away from London, perhaps partly to avoid the confrontation, had urged her mother to keep the constitution.[38] Emmeline Pethick-Lawrence, one of the four newly appointed leaders, later explained that Christabel, as the WSPU's tactical innovator, had 'conceived the militant campaign as a whole' and 'she could not trust her mental offspring to the mercies of politically untrained minds'.[39] Christabel put it rather more bluntly: what if some of the leaders were 'replaced by others of a different point of view!'[40] Those members unable to accept the new structure, including Edith How-Martyn, Teresa Billington and Charlotte Despard, left and formed the Women's Freedom League, a militant and democratic organisation. The WSPU now needed a new political culture to erase labour movement traditions and justify the new 'autocracy'. It seized on the metaphor of the army, where rank and file members dedicated their unquestioning loyalty to unelected leaders. Joan of Arc became the WSPU heroine; the red flags were replaced by a tricolour of purple, white and green to represent the classless ideals of justice, purity and hope, while the socialist songs were replaced first with a 'Women's Marseillaise' and later with 'The March of the Women' whose relentlessly evangelical lyrics ('Hark, hark, hear how it swells / Thunder of freedom, the voice of the Lord!') perfectly captured the WSPU cult of the woman crusader.[41]

After the 1907 split, WSPU members were required to sign a pledge not to support candidates of any political party until after women won the vote – a pledge Sylvia never signed.[42] In the first issue of the WSPU's newspaper, *Votes for Women*, the editorial went even further: 'if you have any class feeling you must leave that behind when you come into this movement. For the women who are in our ranks know no barriers of class distinction.'[43]

That this was followed by an exhortation to have 'no conspiracies, no double dealings in our ranks' and to follow the leaders indicates the extent to which the attack on democracy in the WSPU was linked with the attempt to remove social questions from the struggle. In practice, the claim to be classless in a rigidly class-divided society meant uncritically accepting the status quo. Being part of a 'classless' organisation was clearly far more appealing to women whose socially privileged position was not going to be challenged, than to a working-class woman whose socially inferior position would also remain unchallenged because that was deemed a class issue.

It was not that the suffragette leadership ignored class – they often invoked the starving sweated labourers in their speeches – it was just that the solution to all these problems had to be first and foremost the vote. They presented the vote as a demobilising force, condemning protest by any other groups as an undemocratic indulgence since, if the vote was the solution to all social problems, all they need do was exercise the vote. At a large public meeting in 1908, Christabel argued that male protesters would be wrong even to send a deputation to the House of Commons as the suffragettes did: 'If men took this means of influencing Parliament it would be wrong, and I will tell you why – because they have representatives sitting in the House of Commons.'[44]

Moreover, WSPU evocations of working-class women tended to reflect less the strong workers depicted on Sylvia's early membership card, and increasingly victims whose poverty drove them to child neglect, infanticide and prostitution.[45] That working-class women were potentially powerful if they united at work – as many were to do just a few years later in the Great Unrest (1910–14) – was an unacceptable view to an organisation that excluded solutions based on class. The WSPU's solution to the weakness they perceived in working-class women was articulated by Emmeline Pethick-Lawrence in *Votes for Women* in 1908:

I appeal especially at this moment to the strong to come forward now and take upon their shoulders the burden of the weak. It is not the toiling mother, the sweated worker, the deserted wife, the worsted in life, who can bear the strain and stress of the battle we are fighting for women's deliverance to-day.[46]

This call for middle-class women to fight on behalf of their poorer sisters meant that middle-class women dictated the priorities and tactics, while working-class women were marginalized. Mrs Knight, who had been one of the first London suffragette prisoners in 1906, was by 1907 reporting to her solidly working-class Canning Town branch that on an upcoming demonstration the WSPU leadership insisted that their women 'were to keep in the back ground'. The official reason was that the WSPU could not protect these women from arrest, but it reinforced the trend of removing working-class women from the centre of the campaign. Mrs Knight resigned a week later saying the WSPU 'were not keeping their promises to the working women'. The minute book of the Canning Town branch, the first WSPU branch in London, ends in 1907 with complaints that they had been neglected.[47]

SYLVIA'S QUIET REBELLION

In October 1906 a group of suffragettes, including Sylvia's sister Adela, were arrested after being forced out of the lobby of the House of Commons. Their cases were rushed through a police court where their friends, some of whom wanted to testify as witnesses, were excluded. On hearing this, Sylvia walked into the court and confronted the magistrate. The police threw her onto the street where she attempted to address the crowd, was arrested herself, taken back into the court and sentenced to 14 days in Holloway prison. Only four months later Sylvia participated in a suffragette deputation to Parliament which was met with police violence followed by arrests, and Sylvia was sentenced to a second term in Holloway. Although she had renounced her leadership position, Sylvia was a committed suffragette activist at the forefront of the struggle, but this did not mean that she obeyed the leaders' orders. In prison she had been horrified by the unsanitary conditions – unchanged blankets, the bath water that prisoners had to share – the meagre and unpleasant food, the casual humiliations and the misery of her fellow prisoners.[48] Despite Christabel's instruction 'to ignore the prison conditions, in order to concentrate attention on the vote', Sylvia immediately began to campaign against the poor treatment of prisoners by selling her sketches of life in Holloway to the press.[49] At the breakfast organised to welcome Sylvia on her release from prison the Penal Reform Union was established. She felt it was important 'to secure prison reforms, not for ourselves, but for the ordinary prisoners',[50] which ran directly counter to Christabel's policy of separating the suffragettes from wider struggles.

Sylvia's resistance to the WSPU's political trajectory was also reflected in her personal life. At a time when the WSPU leadership was insisting that its members separate themselves off from political alignment with the Labour Party, Sylvia fell in love with the Labour leader, Keir Hardie. Their relationship not only defied the WSPU but also one of society's cardinal proscriptions since Hardie was married. While Hardie spent most of his time in London, his wife and children lived in his Scottish home, which presumably helped Hardie and Sylvia to distance themselves from them emotionally. Had the relationship been public knowledge the consequences for both of them politically and personally could have been devastating; given the secrecy, little is known about when the relationship began or what kind of a relationship it was. However, the letters they exchanged when Sylvia was abroad in 1911 and 1912 indicate that it was probably a sexual relationship or, at least, that they wanted it to be. Thus a poem in one of her letters to him told of:

> Waiting to feel your kisses on my mouth
> The clasping of your arms and your dear lips
> Pressing on me 'till my breath comes short.
> All I know so well of you, each touch
> Each caress, your breaking under your voice.[51]

Despite a difference in age of 24 years and their different class backgrounds they were united by their shared ideals and each helped the other with their campaigns.

Further evidence of Sylvia's questioning of WSPU strategy can be seen in a tour she undertook in the summer of 1907 in which she interviewed women workers and painted them at their work with the idea of producing 'a book dealing with the work of women in a large number of trades'.[52] Her extensive tour encompassed the chain makers of Cradley Heath, the shoemakers of Leicester, the pit brow 'lassies' of Wigan, the pottery workers in Staffordshire, the fisherwomen of Scarborough, agricultural workers in the Border Counties, and finally cotton workers in a Glasgow mill. The meticulous empirical details she gathered about the women's pay and conditions over a broad range of trades were in marked contrast to the WSPU's evocations of metaphorical or token women workers to excite middle-class pity. The book was never finished (much of it remains only in unpublished typescript, although extracts were published some years later as articles in *Votes for Women*) but her research appeared to point to a conclusion that challenged both those in the labour movement who were attempting to ignore questions of oppression and the WSPU leadership who insisted that questions of class were irrelevant to the women's movement. Instead, Sylvia's work highlighted the importance of both struggles by revealing the devastating interaction of oppression and exploitation on working women's lives. She demonstrated that women in all kinds of trades experienced greater exploitation at work precisely because of discrimination based on sex. Where this inequality extended into the actual labour performed, Sylvia felt that this translated into a general degradation of women workers. She emphasised this difference in men and women's work in her description of potato picking near Berwick, where the plough was driven by a man while

> following in the wake of the plough there was a long line of women stooping and bending, bending and stooping, over the furrows, groping with their hands in the loose soil, and gathering up the potatoes as they came.

> There were three or four men in the field also, the overlookers, who stood talking and smoking by the hedge.[53]

Though Sylvia demonstrates no empathy with the women potato pickers, whom she described as physically repulsive and coarse, she seems to locate the blame for their condition in their inferior treatment by the male workers.[54] By contrast, where men and women worked together she admired their skill and cooperation, observing of the male and female agricultural labourers engaged in cutting corn:

> the woman driver standing up on a wooden bar fastened across the top of the cart has to fork the sheaves far up across her head. High up on the stack a girl catches them as they come swinging through the air and throws them from her to a man, who alternately crawls, kneeling and placing the sheaves carefully round the top of the stack – the heads of grain turned inward and the stalks touching the outer edge, and then stands up and throws the sheaves down on the stack as he catches them to form an inner circle.[55]

There are men and women drivers and they address each other equally 'amid cries of "Wo!" "Back man!" "Back!" "Back woman!"'[56] At a time when the WSPU was trying to separate the women's movement from other struggles, Sylvia's research demonstrated that men and women benefited by working together. Her admiration for the physical strength of the pit-brow women, who unloaded and sorted the coal at the top of coal mine shafts – 'Indeed, when one sees them working side by side with the men, they appear almost stronger than the men'[57] – reads almost as a direct challenge to the WSPU rhetoric, which increasingly portrayed working-class women as weak victims.

Indeed, Sylvia no longer portrayed contemporary working women for WSPU commissions as she had done in 1906. In 1909 she undertook her most ambitious artistic commission for the WSPU, decorating canvases to cover every wall of the large Prince's Skating Rink where a suffragette exhibition was to be held. In harmony with the WSPU's new spiritual aesthetic, the huge designs illustrated a quotation from the Psalms: 'He that goeth forth and weepeth bearing precious seed shall doubtless come again with rejoicing bringing his sheaves with him.' However, the harvesters – who had been recast as women for the Skating Rink designs – were not reminiscent of the harvesting women Sylvia had met two years earlier in the Border Counties. The tunic-clad harvesting women she painted for the WSPU could almost have been figures from an ancient Greek vase or a Pre-Raphaelite painting. The winged angels in the design were a popular motif of Sylvia's used on WSPU books, calendars, banners, cards and other printed literature. The muscular workers standing shoulder to shoulder in her early membership card design would have been clearly inappropriate for the organisation the WSPU had become; yet representing the type of women leading the WSPU as other suffragette propaganda had done (for example, contrasting the enfranchised male idiot or criminal with an unenfranchised, educated lady) would surely have jarred with Sylvia's democratic principles. This may explain why she chose spiritual and allegorical modes of representation. Images of collectivity were now replaced with images of sacrifice, such as the pelican piercing its breast to feed its starving young with its own blood.

Sylvia's rejection of images of contemporary working-class women in her WSPU commissions, but not in her work as an independent artist and writer, reflects the tension between individual self-sacrifice and collective action which Sylvia struggled with throughout the suffragette movement.

MILITANCY AND MASS MOBILISATIONS

From the start the WSPU combined individual acts of heroism, such as facing violent ejection from a Liberal meeting, with protests that larger numbers of women could be involved in, such as demonstrations outside Parliament or Cabinet ministers' houses – which also sometimes resulted in arrests. In June 1908, in response to the comment by Herbert Gladstone, the Home Secretary, that mass assemblies by men had won them the vote but 'of course it cannot be expected that women can assemble in such masses', the WSPU set out to prove him wrong and undermine his argument for denying women the vote.[58] They organised a huge demonstration in Hyde Park on the 21st of June. Estimates of those who attended ranged between 200,000 and 750,000.[59] It was a glorious display of the WSPU's flair for spectacle. Numerous banners, some designed by Sylvia, were especially commissioned; women marched in white dresses adorned with purple and green, converging on Hyde Park in seven separate processions. Leading suffragettes, including Sylvia, spoke to the enormous crowd from the various platforms, and the day culminated in a great shout of 'votes for women'. The Prime Minister, now Herbert Asquith, responded by saying he had 'nothing to add'.[60]

Christabel's reaction was to call for increased militancy to force the government to listen, writing in Votes for Women, 'what really led Parliament to extend the men's franchise was not the conviction that there existed a widespread demand for the vote, but fear of serious consequences should the vote be longer withheld'.[61] A 'widespread demand' and the 'fear of serious consequences' were not, for Christabel, necessarily related. Evidently her view of 'serious consequences' was not drawn from the Chartist movement who tried to make the country ungovernable from below. Instead, Christabel looked to militant action by a very small number of wealthy women. Immediately after Asquith's dismissal of the Hyde Park demonstration, Christabel wrote in Votes for Women, 'it is especially the duty of women of distinction and influence to show their earnestness and devotion to this cause by taking part in the militant movement'.[62]

After the June 30th suffragette protest in Parliament Square was attacked by the police and gangs of thugs, and watched by Cabinet ministers, two suffragettes threw stones at 10 Downing Street and smashed two windows. Though the WSPU leadership had not been informed of this in advance, and the women were hardly of the profile sought by Christabel – Edith New had been a pupil-teacher and Mary Leigh was a working-class radical married to a builder – the WSPU embraced the tactic which expressed the frustrations of the membership at the government's intransigence. However, it also became used as a

means of redefining militancy. One of those arrested at the June
30th protest, Florence Haig, told the police court 'Mr. Asquith
has shown us that peaceful demonstrations are useless.'[63]
Even though the mass action of the Hyde Park demonstration
marked a qualitative break with the older suffragist movement,
Emmeline Pethick-Lawrence now defined it as non-militant: 'the
possibilities of constitutional agitation culminated on June 21st
of this year'.[64] Militancy increasingly meant individual and not
collective action. Marginalizing collective action also meant
rejecting the most effective traditions of the labour movement,
while individual acts of heroism were likely to attract more
attention if performed by a prominent, wealthy woman.

This problem became more apparent with the escalation of
militancy from 1909. In July 1909 suffragette prisoner Marion
Wallace Dunlop went on hunger strike to attempt to force the
authorities to recognise her as a political prisoner by placing
her in the First Division.[*] She was released from prison after
91 hours of fasting. Other suffragette prisoners adopted the
tactic, but in September 1909 the prison authorities refused
to release two hunger strikers. Suffragettes Mary Leigh and
Charlotte Marsh were the first to be force fed. After more than
30 hours in handcuffs in a punishment cell, Mary Leigh was
held down by wardresses while a prison doctor forced a long
tube up her nose down which was poured liquidised food. This
desperately painful and traumatic experience was repeated
twice a day for over a month on Mary Leigh, and for nearly
three months for Charlotte Marsh. But as the force feeding of
suffragettes continued it became harder to keep the prisoners
in the public eye, especially if they were not famous names.
When two suffragettes, Selina Martin and Leslie Hall, hunger
struck while on remand they were treated especially cruelly –
they were force fed and Martin was thrown down stairs and
put in a straitjacket – but the WSPU struggled to get any press

---

[*]   There were three categories of prisoners. Those recognised as political
prisoners were sentenced to the First Division, but the suffragettes were
frequently sentenced to the Second and Third Divisions reserved for common
criminals, where their treatment was harsher.

attention.[65] Mary Gawthorpe explained the problem to fellow suffragette Lady Constance Lytton: 'with tears in her eyes, as she threw her arms round me: "Oh, and these are women quite unknown – nobody knows or cares about them except their own friends. They go to prison again and again to be treated like this, until it kills them!"'[66]

Constance Lytton, a member of one of Britain's most famous aristocratic families, had herself been a hunger-striking suffragette prisoner but had never been force fed, the authorities saying it would be too dangerous for her weak heart. In response to Martin's treatment, Lytton now went to prison disguised as 'Jane Warton', a working-class woman. This time her heart was not tested and she was force fed repeatedly until her identity became known and she was hurriedly released.* The huge publicity her action achieved exposed the class bias of the prison authorities and the press. But she was only able to expose this precisely because she was really Lady Constance Lytton and not Jane Warton.

SYLVIA ON THE MARGINS

Throughout this period Sylvia's opposition to the WSPU leadership took a very individualised form: abandoning the honorary secretary position on her own terms, refusing to sign the pledge, her relationship with Hardie, even her research into women's work which she conducted alone. This reflected the fact that she did not perceive herself as a suffragette leader and so she made no attempts to organise a different strategy. Therefore she did not try to link up with those suffragettes whose conception of militancy was closer to her own. She did not, perhaps out of a sense of family loyalty, join with the women clamouring for democracy in the WSPU in 1907, nor with the disgruntled Canning Town branch. At the beginning of 1907, her younger

---

* Constance Lytton paid a high price for her courageous action. She suffered a heart attack in 1912 which left her partially paralysed. She died, never having recovered her health, in 1923, aged 54.

sister Adela was attempting to link up the suffragettes in Hebden Bridge with striking weavers, yet Sylvia was not engaged in this experiment of uniting the women's movement with a labour dispute.[67]

Sylvia's somewhat marginal role was partly due to personal tragedy. In late 1909, when her beloved brother Harry developed paralysis, Sylvia spent the winter nursing him. But Harry was terminally ill and died on the 5th of January 1910. Her mother's decision that it should be Sylvia who would stop work and care for her brother was probably because Sylvia was the least active family member in the campaign, but it also echoed other decisions by her mother and sister which resulted in Sylvia being kept away from the centre of the movement. Although Sylvia felt a moral obligation to undergo force feeding, telling Hardie 'I shall have to go to prison to stand by the others', she was unable to do so at first because she was nursing Harry and then because she was commissioned to write a history of the suffragettes.[68] Her book, *The Suffragette: The History of the Women's Militant Suffrage Movement 1905–1910*, loyally reproduced the leadership's official version of history. This commission kept her away from the limelight and forced her to suppress her growing criticisms, but when a publicity tour for the book was organised in America at the beginning of 1911, Sylvia was confronted as a leading British suffragette with questions about how the women's movement should relate to the issues of class and racial oppression.[69] Freed from the restrictive dilemmas at home, Sylvia's answers would have far-reaching consequences.

3

Working For Their Own Emancipation

CLASS, RACE AND SOCIALISM IN THE UNITED STATES

Sylvia undertook two American tours, one in 1911 and one in 1912. The tours were long and arduous; as Sylvia later remembered: 'I travelled almost every night, and spoke once, twice or thrice a day.'[1] In her three-month-long 1911 tour she went from New York to St. Paul in Minnesota, Chicago and Evanston in Illinois, Kansas City, St. Louis, Indianapolis and Detroit, before speaking in Ottawa and Toronto in Canada. After more New York meetings, she travelled to the other side of the United States, stopping in Denver, Los Angeles and San Francisco before returning west, stopping in Albany, Concord and Boston. Keir Hardie thought the schedule 'clearly impossible'.[2] Some meetings were of great historical significance: she was the second woman to address the Senate and House of Representatives in joint convention, the first having been the famous American feminist Susan B. Anthony; she was the first woman to address the City Club in St. Louis and the first to address the Michigan Legislature.[3] She addressed the Colorado and Iowa Legislatures, spoke in New York's huge Carnegie Hall, and debated in Boston's State Hall.[4] Though she lacked her mother's impeccably elegant appearance – the *Chicago Sunday Tribune* noted 'she is not bothered about her hair, nor the hang of her skirt' – she nonetheless impressed audiences with her sincere and well-informed speeches.[5] A Los Angeles newspaper stated that she delivered 'a talk that for ingenuity and wit and real dramatic effect has rarely been equalled'.[6] An Indianapolis reporter was struck by the slender slip of a girl who stood up on the big platform, pleadingly holding out her hands, and looking in her girlish isolation very lonely. But make no mistake: there was neither loneliness nor helplessness. There was a girl who knew what she was talking about; and she was talking about it exceedingly well.[7]

She spoke to 19,000 at Denver, and in Boston so many people turned up to hear her that three overflow meetings were formed.[8]

But Sylvia was determined to push her tours beyond the fundraising ventures like those her mother undertook in America, in which middle-class American suffrage supporters entertained their guest at elegant social functions. Sylvia sought to link the struggle for women's rights to some of the most oppressed and exploited sections of American society. Arriving in New York in 1911 she hastened to meet a group of laundry workers taking strike action. Sylvia was impressed by the dramatic effect the strike had upon previously unorganised workers: 'When the strike began on New Year's Day 1911, the laundry workers, two-thirds of whom were said to be women and girls, and one-third men, were quite unorganised, but a Trade Union was quickly formed, and the workers joined in large numbers.'[9]

Strikers marched through the streets quickly spreading the action. One woman told Sylvia 'she had been at work in the laundry when a procession of strikers went past. She had stopped work at once, but the doors were locked, and she was told that she could not go. She had then picked up an iron bar, and declared that she would fight her way out.'[10] The spirit of the striking laundry workers, and the police repression they faced, made it easy for them and the English suffragette to identify with each other's struggle. Sylvia arrived at a strikers' meeting where

a bouquet of flowers was just being presented to a woman, an American citizen, just released from prison – one of the strike pickets who was to be tried for obstruction, and who had been arrested and kept in prison for two days before bail could be procured. She replied in a short speech, which was received with great cheering, and immediately afterwards an enthusiastic welcome was given to a negro man strike picket, who was also released from prison that day. Then an Italian, speaking with impassioned eloquence in his native tongue, as a stimulus and encouragement to all present, called upon them to remember the hundreds of British women who have suffered violence and imprisonment in the cause of their Enfranchisement.[11]

She also visited Harrison Street Gaol in Chicago, prisons in Ottawa and New York, the juvenile courts and a detention centre in Colorado. In Los Angeles she spoke to striking women factory workers before returning to New York where she found a changed atmosphere. On the 25th of March 1911 a fire had swept through the Triangle Shirtwaist Company building and the workers, mostly women, found themselves trapped: the company regularly locked the doors to stop its workers taking breaks; 146 workers were killed.[12] Sylvia attended the memorial procession, 'a sad day of mourning, when rain poured from a grey sky, and a long procession of saddened workgirls marched in their poor black garments, to show honour and respect to their comrades burnt to death in an awful fire'.[13]

It was probably here that Sylvia met Rose Schneiderman, the Polish Jewish immigrant trade union organiser who had been a garment worker herself, and who was involved with the memorial. Schneiderman also campaigned for women's suffrage, which perhaps reinforced Sylvia's belief that there could be unity between the labour and suffrage movements.

Sylvia was also intensely aware of race in the United States. In her depiction of the laundry strikers' meeting she celebrated the unity of the woman worker with a black worker and Italian immigrant worker. However, she did not find this spirit of unity across the American women's movement, something she confronted head-on at the Women's City Club in Missouri where *Votes for Women* reported that she

created something of a sensation by telling her hearers that they were no further advanced than the Chinese and the Turks whom they held in contempt. 'You are,' said Miss Pankhurst, 'the most backward nation in the Western world, and here in Missouri you have the most backward State.' She cited cases to prove her statement and showed that the evils

resulting from low wages and the unjust economic conditions under which
women lived in that city were worse than existed elsewhere.[14]

It was probably around this point that she made her most radical
departure from the pre-planned tour schedule. One of her letters
to Hardie indicates that the decision was deliberately rebellious:
'I have determined to go South where no one ever goes much
where Mother did not go and where above all things there
is so much much to do [sic]. Awful conditions of labour for
women and children especially children and everything generally
backward.'[15]

Travelling through the New Mexico desert she saw the
reservations the Native Americans had been forced onto. She
was disgusted when a businessman told her that he paid Native
American women a pittance to produce traditional rugs, which
he then sold for a huge profit, while the impoverished Native
Americans could only afford 'cheap machine-made things'.
Visiting the Indian College in Kansas she found the students
were taught skills needed for mass-production factory goods,
bearing no trace of their cultural heritage:

> So the crafts and the decorative arts are dying out through poverty and
> disease in the reservations, and they are being stamped out, even more
> absolutely, by contact with commerce-made ugliness and false standards
> in schools and colleges. Soon, those sharp Yankee hustlers will have no
> more Indian wares to make their money with.[16]

Sylvia's visit to an Indian College was in itself a radical decision,
but her refusal to take the institution at face-value and her
indictment of the effect of racism and capitalism on culture
indicates that she identified with the Native Americans, perhaps
particularly as a fellow artist.

She also went to Nashville in Tennessee where she was
horrified to hear 'members of old Nashville families ... talk
glibly of the "slavery" days" [sic] as they sit behind the Negro
coachman, or are waited on at table by the Negro women
servants'.[17] Visiting the local prison she was sickened by the foul
conditions and virulent racism: the superintendent told her 'the

present treatment of negroes was too lenient, "We ought to burn them!"'[18] Most controversially she addressed a black audience at Tennessee's Negro University: 'I was astonished to find every newspaper I opened on my journey thither, protesting against my action.'[19] She evidently conveyed the suffragette struggle for freedom in a way that this audience particularly could relate to, for she felt 'they seemed to listen more intently than other audiences'.[20] Sylvia's approach was therefore fundamentally different from her mother's who, addressing a black American audience in 1913, 'aroused the volatile emotions of the coloured women by picturing the good they could accomplish for their race by working for the reforms their white sisters advocated'.[21]

Emmeline could see no place for the struggles of oppressed groups within the suffragette struggle, whereas Sylvia's decisions about her tour indicate that she saw the fight for women's rights as a fight that should identify with all oppressed groups, from laundry workers to Native and black Americans. Sylvia's detailed exploration of racism, public institutions and labour conditions made her tour the most radical undertaken by an English suffragette.

It was also in America that she developed her ideas about what kind of struggle resulted in genuine emancipation. Hearing that the city of Milwaukee in Wisconsin was run by a socialist administration, she was eager to see how socialism might work in practice. However, she was largely disappointed by what she saw. Inspecting a model laundry, Sylvia noted 'the workers were absolutely silent. They seemed just a part of the machinery.' She felt the priority was efficiency, rather than improving workers' lives. In particular, she objected to the notion that a few could create socialism on behalf of the rest. It was an attitude the city's Mayor, Emile Sidel, adopted with regard to women. When he told Sylvia that proclaiming socialism would render the fight for votes for women irrelevant, she argued back 'women need their votes to fight for better conditions just as men do. It is strange how few even of the best of men can quite see that we need the power to work out our own salvation as much as they do.'[22] As historian Les Garner has argued, it was through observing an existing model of 'socialism' that Sylvia began to explicitly articulate her own conception of 'socialism from below': that liberation could not be handed down from above, but could only be won by people being involved in the struggle for it themselves.[23] This would have far-reaching consequences for Sylvia's critique of the British women's suffrage movement.

THE WSPU AND THE GREAT UNREST

Less than two months after Sylvia's return to England in April 1911, a strike wave erupted across the docks. The WSPU claimed their own militancy was superior to the 'male' industrial unrest, and their cause more valid: 'the Suffragists have far greater reason for their revolt against the existing order of things. In the first place, working men have votes, and by greater skill in their manipulation could gain improvements in their condition without resorting to strikes.'[24] Where once the WSPU saw the vote as a tool in a wider struggle, it was rapidly becoming a panacea. Instead of denouncing the employers who had plunged working-class families into intolerable poverty, *Votes for Women* blamed the workers fighting back for the increased burden the strike imposed on their wives:

> Women's part in the strike has been mainly this – they have paid the greater part of the price and have endured the greater part of the suffering. For the men on strike, the interest and the joy of conflict. For their wives, the troubles which visit the housewife when the cupboard is bare and the children cry to be fed and when the present lack of the weekly income brings a burden of debt to landlord and pawnbroker, which must be repaid as the result of her self-denial in the future.[25]

The WSPU, which celebrated self-denial and sacrifice, could see no heroism in the Great Unrest. Their insistence that the striker and his wife had different interests was put under considerable strain when unorganised factory workers around the Bermondsey docks – many of whom were dockers' wives and daughters – also walked out of work in August 1911. Marching through the streets singing 'Fall in and follow me', increasing numbers of women joined them.[26] This was not a strike over one specific grievance, it was a tide of rage against the way they were treated every day of their lives: paid poverty wages, reduced even further by punitive fines, they had to rush around carrying huge vats of boiling jam in notoriously dangerous conditions.[27] Pink's jam factory workers summed it up on their banner thus: 'We are not white slaves, but Pink's slaves'.[28] Fighting back transformed these women; suddenly they were confident of their own power:

> The women seemed to be in the highest spirits. They went laughing and singing through Bermondsey, shouting 'Are we downhearted?' and answering the question by a shrill chorus of 'No!' it was noticeable that many of them had put on their 'Sunday best.' In spite of the great heat, hundreds of them wore fur boas and tippets – the sign of self-respect.[29]

They joined the National Federation of Women Workers in their thousands and in most cases they won wage increases.[30]

Votes for Women, while not condemning the strike, preached that the solution to starvation wages 'is the Parliamentary vote', thereby dismissing the rather more immediate solutions being posed by the victims of starvation wages themselves.[31] The WSPU leadership made no attempt to bring these women into the suffrage campaign, implying that the 'solution' to these women's problems lay not in their own hands, but in the hands of others.

REPRESENTING WORKING WOMEN

Once again, Sylvia rebelled and made her way to Bermondsey not to talk *at* the women, or tell them that all they needed was the vote, but to get them to talk to her about their lives: 'I questioned fully three hundred women as to their average weekly wages.'[32] That she was drawn to the women's strike suggests Sylvia had identified that the WSPU might have drawn new energy from another group of women who were just discovering the power of collective protest. However, she did not at this point have the confidence or platform to argue this within the WSPU – in fact she kept her visit to the Bermondsey strikers quiet until a year later, when Christabel was out of the country.

The tension was perhaps best expressed in her art. Late in 1911 Sylvia provided the artistic spectacle for the WSPU's Christmas Fair. The canvases she had painted for the Skating Rink in 1909 were re-used to cover the walls, but the theme she chose for 1911 was in stark contrast with the spiritual, classless aesthetic she had created two years before. She designed stallholders' costumes based on late eighteenth and early nineteenth-century peasant clothes. She explained in *Votes for Women*: 'This was an epoch of great change; new ideas of freedom were everywhere in the air. It was the time of the French Revolution.'[33] If Sylvia could no longer depict contemporary workers for the suffragettes, she could get away with depicting working women of the past.

REBUILDING THE MOVEMENT

Sylvia faced a very different atmosphere when she returned from America in April 1912. The WSPU had abstained from militancy, declaring a 'truce', to aid the passage of the Conciliation Bill, which would have enfranchised a narrow section of women. When the Conciliation Bill was due to come before Parliament early in 1912, the government suddenly introduced its own Reform Bill – to enfranchise more men – and women would only be included if a separate amendment was introduced and passed. The WSPU saw it as an attempt to eclipse the Conciliation Bill and the return to militancy was announced when Emmeline Pankhurst declared 'the argument of the broken pane is the most valuable argument in modern politics'.[34] On the 1st and 4th of March 1912 suffragettes strolled down the fashionable West End streets before pulling hammers from their handbags and smashing the famous department stores' windows. Hundreds of women were arrested and thousands of pounds worth of damage had been done.

The WSPU leadership were to be charged with conspiracy to commit damage to property. Such a serious charge would carry long sentences. Emmeline Pankhurst, and Emmeline and

Frederick Pethick-Lawrence were arrested, but the police could not find Christabel. Convinced that she was the movement's best leader, Christabel saw it as vitally important that she remained free.[35] In the dead of night she took taxis across London and was hidden by friends who burned her distinctive hat and provided her with new clothes. The next morning a woman calling herself Amy Richards boarded the boat train for France and Christabel Pankhurst was free.

Sylvia felt the WSPU was pursuing completely the wrong course of action. With the leaders facing long prison terms what was needed was a renewed campaign to win popular support and a broader base of activists: 'a large popular agitation for the vote itself must be maintained at fever heat, and the fate of the prisoners always kept in the public eye'. Instead, the WSPU was secretly organising small, select groups of women to commit increasingly militant acts, an unsustainable policy which threatened to alienate the public, providing little reason for them to care about the fate of the prisoners. She travelled, in disguise, to meet Christabel in Paris where she found the differences between them more pronounced than ever. Sylvia's concerns found no resonance with her sister. She discouraged Sylvia's involvement, advising her to 'behave as though you were not in the country!' However, Sylvia, especially after her American experiences, was increasingly confident of her own analysis and she concluded that Christabel's refusal to give her any specific tasks could be used to her strategic advantage as it 'would leave me the more free to do what I thought necessary in my own way'.[36]

Sylvia argued for a return to demonstrations to win back public support. Throughout the summer of 1912 Sylvia's ideas dominated suffragette activity in London. When nine-month sentences were handed to Emmeline Pankhurst and the Pethick-Lawrences, Sylvia threw herself into organising the biggest suffragette demonstrations since the historic 1908 Hyde Park demonstration. There were at least 12,000 people at Wimbledon, 15,000 in Regents Park and 30,000 in Blackheath. Labour politicians spoke on the platforms alongside suffragettes. Street corner meetings were planned to coincide with workers' dinner

hours and the end of the working day.[37] The suffragettes, who
a year earlier had largely ignored the Bermondsey strikers, were
now sent there to agitate and found the women receptive to
linking the struggles, as they 'realise that the ends for which they
were willing and ready to suffer were also the ends for which
the women of the W.S.P.U were willing and ready to suffer'.[38]
Sylvia increasingly defined the women's suffrage struggle in class
terms. Comparing the suffragettes to Wat Tyler's struggle against
serfdom, she depicted the suffragettes on the side of the poor,
fighting against the privileged classes: 'the House of Commons
– the best club in London ... the Cabinet Ministers in their velvet
coats and gold lace, their salaries only paid in thousands'.[39] The
campaign culminated in a huge Hyde Park demonstration on the
14th of July – Mrs Pankhurst's birthday. Sylvia's influence was
everywhere in evidence. The socialist colour red, the colour of
the London WSPU's first banner in 1905, was now re-introduced
to the purple, white and green as Sylvia added red caps of liberty
to sit on top of the tricolour banners. The caps themselves were
a reminder of the working-class battle for political rights at
Peterloo in 1819.

THE EAST LONDON FEDERATION

In the autumn of 1912 Sylvia persuaded West London militants
to campaign in London's impoverished East End. As in 1905,
she chose this area to rebuild the women's movement because it
was the 'greatest homogeneous working-class area accessible to
the House of Commons by popular demonstrations'.[40] She also
saw that 'the existence of a strong, self-reliant' working-class
movement would be the best defence against any more attempts
to support Franchise Bills which excluded working-class women;
and she now looked to establish campaigns that would continue
after the vote was won. In words that echoed her reply to
the Milwaukee Mayor, defending liberation from below, she
later recalled:

> I wanted to rouse these women of the submerged mass to be, not merely
> the argument of more fortunate people, but to be fighters on their own
> account, despising mere platitudes and catch-cries, revolting against the
> hideous conditions about them, and demanding for themselves and their
> families a full share of the benefits of civilization and progress.[41]

The local newspaper's announcement that 'arrangements have
already been made for W.S.P.U. speakers to address thirty-six
branches of Trades Unions of men and women'[42] indicates
the extent to which this campaign defied Christabel's policy.
Headquarters of what became known as the East London
Federation (ELF) of the WSPU were established in former shops
on prominent East London streets: Bow Road, Roman Road and
the East India Dock Road.

Their early street meetings were frequently disrupted;
fireworks, fish heads and paper soaked in urinals were thrown
at suffragette speakers.[43] Sylvia's prominence made her a
favourite target: 'I was never free from numerous bruises.'[44]
However, many local women were already on their side. 'At
all our meetings women, especially elderly women, indignantly
protest against interruptions, and sometimes even push men who
make disagreeable remarks out of the crowd.'[45]

Sylvia met one woman who during the transport strike
punched a strike breaker who had assaulted her husband on
the picket line. Sent to Holloway, she was proud to have been
sentenced to four days solitary confinement on bread and water
for playing football with a suffragette prisoner.[46]

The suffragettes campaigned tirelessly, organising a huge
series of street meetings: over a period of six days they held
an average of just over five meetings every night.[47] At least
part of the hostility they encountered was motivated by the
perception 'that we only wanted votes for propertied women
and cared nothing for the poor'.[48] Sylvia began to dispel this
impression, as she had done in Bermondsey, by persuading the
working women to tell her about their grievances which she
would then report in her articles. In this way she began to make
the vote relevant to these women by specifically linking it with
the problems that they wanted to change. East End suffragettes

would later cite Sylvia's working-class focus as an important reason for their own involvement. Annie Barnes, who joined in her early twenties, recalled:

> [Sylvia] wasn't like her mother. Mrs Pankhurst and her friends were only interested in getting the vote for rich women. But Sylvia disagreed with her. 'My father launched the campaign for women, *all* women,' she said. 'And I'm carrying it on.' And she came to the East End ... and formed the East London Federation of Suffragettes. That's what I joined.'[49]

Many of the new activists were linked to the labour movement. Young Elsie Lagsding, from a Labour family, who went into domestic service at 14 and trained as a cook, first encountered Sylvia speaking from the ELF shop in the East India Dock Road: 'so my friend and I we stood outside listening for a while, then she invited them in, "come in" you know, so I said come on in, come and hear what she's got so say, we went in, we walked in. In the evening it was, and then after a bit of a talk and that, we said we'd join, so we both joined up.'[50] Melvina Walker, the wife of a docker who had participated in the dock strike, became one of the ELF's most able public speakers.[51] Annie Lake was a member of the National Federation of Women Workers. Factory worker Elsie Taylor, who joined the ELF as a teenager, was a Tailor and Garment Workers' Union member and, unofficially but by popular acclaim, the spokeswoman for her fellow workers. She joined the Social Democratic Federation at 16 (the earliest age they would take members) and was a member of the Clarion cycling club.[52] Many of these women thus saw the ELF's brand of suffragism as entirely compatible with their involvement in socialist and working-class organisations.

'WOMEN'S WAR' ON LABOUR

The links with the labour movement that Sylvia was building were threatened by Christabel's announcement in 1912 that 'a women's war upon the Parliamentary Labour Party is inevitable'[53] unless Labour MPs agreed to vote against every measure the Liberals put forward in Parliament. Dismissing the fact that Labour did not have enough MPs to block Liberal measures, the demand reflected Christabel's prioritisation of women's suffrage *above all other progressive causes*, rather than attempting to make common cause with them. Refusing to recognise the oppression the British government was inflicting in Ireland, she argued that Labour should even vote against Home Rule for Ireland, as the Irish 'are already represented in the Imperial Parliament'.[54] Where Sylvia saw other progressive movements as fighting the same enemy as the suffragettes, and therefore as potential allies, Christabel saw them only as rivals.

There may also have been darker motives behind Christabel's new policy. In the spring of 1912 the suffragist NUWSS made an electoral pact with the Labour Party, declaring they would support pro-women's suffrage Labour candidates while in return Labour, at its 1913 conference, agreed not to support any enfranchisement bill that did not include women.[55] By making an impossible demand of the Labour Party when a possible demand was being forged, Christabel threatened to split the suffrage forces and damage a growing alliance. At the very time Labour were showing signs of challenging the Liberals on this issue, Christabel claimed Labour were in such 'servitude' to the Liberals that only the return of a Conservative government would see them back women's suffrage.[56]

One of the few in the Labour Party who agreed with Christabel's policy was George Lansbury, a Labour MP in East London who was passionately committed to women's suffrage and decided in the autumn of 1912 to resign his seat and re-stand on the question of women's suffrage, turning the election into a kind of referendum. Sylvia regarded it as a terrible mistake. The decision was imposed from above, not generated organically from the alliances that were being built on the ground, indeed Lansbury had not even consulted his local Party branch or the local suffragettes; he made the decision while visiting Christabel in Paris. Though Sylvia was organising in the East End, the WSPU handed control of the election campaign to Grace Roe, a politically conservative member from outside the area. This reflected the leadership's desire to see Lansbury's return purely as a victory for the suffragettes and not for suffragism and Labour united. Many Labour supporters blamed the suffragettes for Lansbury jeopardising his seat, while Roe's refusal to 'work under the men' meant that the WSPU cars for ferrying voters to the polling station lay idle as the suffragettes would not lend them to Labour, while Labour would not supply the WSPU with the list of voters. In the end Lansbury lost his seat.

Some historians argue that the WSPU's lack of democracy was corrected by a significant degree of autonomy in its local branches.[57] However, the Lansbury by-election demonstrates the extent to which local suffragettes could be overridden at any point, and the way in which national strategy could swiftly threaten delicately constructed alliances. And as soon as local freedoms threatened to alter national strategy they were not tolerated. That summer, Emmeline and Christabel extracted a promise from Adela Pankhurst, who had long pursued an independent strategy, that she would never speak on behalf of the WSPU again.[58] That autumn they expelled the Pethick-Lawrences, who were expressing doubts about escalating militancy.

MARTYRDOM AND THE MASS MOVEMENT

By 1913 the suffragettes were in the contradictory position of undertaking the greatest acts of sacrifice at the time they were making least appeal to public support. Sacrificial extroversion accompanied political introversion. They now spurned popular support. At the end of 1912 *The Suffragette*'s[*] front page carried an open letter 'To the British Public' defending suffragette arson attacks on post boxes thus:

> There are two ways of moving you to action. One is to stir your emotions by means of some appalling tragedy, dramatically described for you by the Press. The other is to make you thoroughly uncomfortable. The more effective of these two ways is to make you uncomfortable![59]

---

[*]   Edited by Christabel it replaced *Votes for Women* as the WSPU organ.

In the end suffragettes resorted to both. The appalling tragedy came in June 1913 when Emily Wilding Davison, with the suffragette colours sewn into her coat, ran in front of the King's horse at the Derby, was knocked down and killed. That same year also saw a spate of suffragette arson attacks, not just on pillar boxes but also empty buildings. Because of the long prison sentences arson carried, these suffragettes tended to operate in secret to avoid arrest. Sylvia felt this 'secret militancy' further alienated the public: 'That secret militancy was really a supreme sacrifice on the part of those who carried it out, was not always plain to outsiders who, not realising its dangers and hardships, thought only that the secret militant did her deed and sought to get away unpunished.'[60] Instead Sylvia felt that 'open militancy', where suffragettes gave themselves up for arrest, could compliment the building of a mass movement, something she tried to put into practice when she called a protest in the East End on the 17th of February 1913 and smashed an undertaker's window, for which she was imprisoned. She saw this protest as

Sylvia continues to work while recovering from a hunger strike in 1913 in the home she shared with Mr and Mrs Payne in the East End's Old Ford Road.

'the beginning of the mass movement for Votes for Women in East London'.[61] Certainly her imprisonment galvanised protests – after long days at work ELF supporters would march miles from the East End to Holloway. Elsie Lagsding remembered it as 'a shocking walk – all mud and slosh you know and icy snow melting'.[62]

Sylvia went further than other suffragette prisoners by going on a thirst strike as well as hunger strike. She soon became the first and only member of the Pankhurst family to endure forcible feeding, which she later graphically described:

> Someone seized me by the head and thrust a sheet under my chin. My eyes were shut. I set my teeth and tightened my lips over them with all my strength. A man's hands were trying to force open my mouth; my breath was coming so fast that I felt as though I should suffocate. His fingers were striving to pull my lips apart – getting inside. I felt them and a steel instrument pressing round my gums, feeling for gaps in my teeth. I was trying to jerk my head away, trying to wrench it free. Two of them were holding it, two of them dragging at my mouth. I was panting and heaving, my breath quicker and quicker, coming now with a low scream which was growing louder. 'Here is a gap,' one of them said. 'No, here is a better one. This long gap here!' A steel instrument pressed my gums, cutting into the flesh. I braced myself to resist that terrible pain. 'No, that won't do' – that voice again. 'Give me the pointed one!' A stab of sharp, intolerable agony. I wrenched my head free. Again they grasped me. Again the struggle. Again the steel cutting its way in, though I strained my force against it. Then something gradually forced my jaws apart as a screw was turned; the pain was like having the teeth drawn. They were trying to get the tube down my throat, I was struggling madly to stiffen my muscles and close my throat. They got it down, I suppose, though I was unconscious of anything then save a mad revolt of struggling, for they said at last: 'That's all!' and I vomited as the tube came up. They left me on the bed exhausted, gasping for breath and sobbing convulsively.[63]

This struggle took place twice a day for over a month. Her gums were constantly bleeding and she often fainted afterwards. Once she was 'sick all over my face and I couldn't get rid of the phlegm' which felt like suffocation.[64] The effects were degrading:

constipation, flatulence and foul-smelling breath.[65] At first she was terrified of going mad.[66] Determined not to take the food, after each feeding she would push her hand down her throat to make herself sick. Her lips became 'cracked and dark' and the blood vessels in her eyes had burst making them look like 'cups of blood'.[67] To force her release she began a 'rest strike', feverishly 'dashing across and across my cell with outstretched arms, throwing my weight against the wall as I turned'.[68] Sylvia walked continuously for 28 hours before the doctors agreed to an independent medical examination and then her release.

While her imprisonment inspired protest in the East End, she had not managed, as she had hoped, to avoid the problem of the privileging of the 'leaders' over the rank and file that individualistic tactics engendered. Zelie Emerson, who had been imprisoned along with Sylvia and also adopted the hunger and thirst strike, had suffered even more desperately: 'She had tried to commit suicide by cutting an artery. She had dug into the flesh with her small, blunt penknife, till she reached the artery, but when she had tried to cut it, she found it, she said, too tough, and like an indiarubber band.'[69] Despite this, Zelie was kept in prison longer than Sylvia, her case attracting a lot less public attention.

Sylvia's actions were perhaps also partly a claim to leadership of the suffragette struggle. In the WSPU, prominence and respect were won by going to prison and undergoing force feeding, and Sylvia's intense involvement was in marked contrast with Christabel's absence. Her attempt to play a greater leadership role in the suffragette struggle also took its toll on her relationship with Hardie. When he came to see her after her release from prison she 'told him it was too painful, too incongruous he should come in the midst of the warfare waged against him and the Labour Party by the orders of my sister'.[70]

FIGHTING BACK: THE PEOPLE'S ARMY

To stop women starving themselves out of their prison sentences, the government introduced the Prisoner's Temporary Discharge for Ill-Health Act whereby the prisoner would be released on licence once she had become dangerously ill and then re-arrested once she was considered well enough to continue her sentence. The suffragettes resisted by evading re-arrest, dubbing the measure a 'Cat and Mouse Act' in which the suffragette mice were hunted down.

When Sylvia fell under the Cat and Mouse Act her attempts to evade arrest offered the opportunity to put into practice the kind of mass resistance she had been working towards. Now she had to rely on the audiences at meetings to protect her from re-arrest. On the occasions she was arrested, she would hunger, thirst and rest strike until release which provided another opportunity for a mass meeting. Sylvia now completely threw her lot in with the East End movement, moving in with Mr and Mrs Payne, shoemakers living on the Old Ford Road. She increasingly won locally organised protection against the police. At an ELF meeting in October 1913 audience members fought with police who brutally attacked the meeting: the ELF's Hackney branch secretary's collar bone was broken, Mary Leigh was beaten unconscious, Zelie Emerson's skull was fractured and another suffragette had her arm broken. When the Poplar Borough Council banned ELF meetings, the ELF were able to mobilise wider working-class support: in December 1913 an ELF demonstration outside one hostile Poplar councillor's home was led by the band of the Gas Workers' Union.[71] Elsie Lagsding, who was on the demonstration, remembered the spirit of unity, 'all the men used to join in as well'.[72] The demonstration was attacked by mounted police who destroyed the band's instruments, beat the protesters, and pursued them into the gardens where they sought refuge. One old woman who witnessed this collapsed on the spot and died.[73]

Sylvia looked to other movements for inspiration. In 1913 police were attacking the Dublin workers locked out of work by their employers in an attempt to make them renounce their membership of the Irish Transport and General Workers Union (ITGWU). To defend themselves against the violence they formed a workers' militia, the Irish Citizen Army. Sylvia formed a 'People's Army' shortly after, enthusiastically drilled by her friend Norah Smyth.[74] The People's Army, which enlisted women alongside men, was immediately formed to protect suffragettes, but, as Sylvia's comments to one involved in the Irish Citizen Army show, it was also intended to defend the organised working class: 'the army must be distinctly to fight for the vote and to protect suffragist prisoners as well as for use in Trade Disputes'.[75]

THE SPLIT

In late 1913 James Larkin, the ITGWU's fiery general secretary, was imprisoned as a result of his role in the Dublin lockout, and Lansbury's *Daily Herald* called a solidarity rally at the Albert Hall. Sylvia was one of the speakers. However, her attendance at the rally clashed with Christabel's support for the Ulster Loyalists, which she claimed was based on their promise (which lasted just six months) that an Ulster state would grant votes for women.[76] In fact, this reflected her increasingly rightwing politics. The republicans were far more natural allies – the ITGWU supported the suffragettes and its socialist leaders were committed on principle to women's suffrage.[77] At the Albert Hall, Larkin's replacement general secretary, the socialist James Connolly, spoke of their common struggle 'against the domination of nation over nation, class over class, and sex over sex'.[78] Indeed, Christabel's position was an anomaly in the wider militant suffrage movement; suffrage activists Dora Montefiore, Fred Pethick-Lawrence and Charlotte Despard also spoke at the Albert Hall meeting. The meeting touched a chord in the women's movement; it was reported 'quite a large percentage of the audience were women, many of whom wore Suffrage badges and sashes'.[79] As the *Daily Herald* was based in the East End it is fair to assume that many of the suffragettes present would have been ELF supporters; certainly the red caps of liberty, worn by the hundred women collecting money for the strike, were a friendly nod to the ELF's traditions.[80] Sylvia, who had to evade the police to attend, called on men and women to fight together: 'Revolt was imperative ... In the Labour movement women were wanted as well as men.'[81]

It was not only the political tone of the meeting that would
have alarmed Christabel but also Sylvia's reported popularity
with the audience, who broke out into a spontaneous call for
Sylvia to speak 'but for some time [she] could not be heard,
owing to the enthusiastic reception accorded her'.[82] One of the
most popular speakers that night, she recalled being cheered
louder even than Connolly 'because of my immediate liability to
arrest'.[83] Sylvia's status as a 'mouse', bravely defying the police by
appearing on public platforms, captured the public imagination
in a way that Christabel's near two-year distant and comfortable
exile could not. In January 1914 Sylvia was summoned to Paris.
'Miserably ill in body' after a recent imprisonment, Sylvia went
with Norah Smyth to see Emmeline and Christabel in Paris,
where Christabel demanded the ELF sever completely from the
WSPU.[84] Apparently when they were alone together Christabel
told Sylvia they should meet 'not as Suffragettes, but as sisters'.
For Sylvia 'the words seemed meaningless; we had no life apart
from the movement'. Indeed, five days before the split with
Sylvia was announced, Adela bowed to her mother's wishes to
stay away from the suffrage movement and boarded a boat for
Australia never to return. Sylvia remembered her father telling
his children 'You are the four pillars of my house!'[85] Now all
the pillars were irrevocably wrenched apart, and the sisters were
never to resume family relationships. Although the split was
unlikely to have come as much of a surprise, Sylvia felt 'bruised,
as one does, when fighting the foe without, one is struck by the
friend within'.[86] Her mother's assessment of her came in the
form of a letter: 'You are unreasonable[,] always have been[,]
and[,] I fear[,] always will be. I suppose you were made so!'[87]

SELF-EMANCIPATION:
THE EAST LONDON FEDERATION OF THE SUFFRAGETTES

According to Sylvia, Christabel told her in Paris that

a working women's movement was of no value: working women were the
weakest portion of the sex: how could it be otherwise? Their lives were too

hard, their education too meagre to equip them for the contest. 'Surely it
is a mistake to use the weakest for the struggle! We want picked women,
the very strongest and most intelligent!'[88]

This view that all the strength and intelligence were gathered
in one section of the population – and not the portion that
did the work – echoed contemporary preoccupations with the
future of 'the race'. These were fears for the values, culture
and privileged status of the people who ran the Empire: white,
Anglo-Saxon, Church of England upper- and middle-class
men. Without challenging its fundamentally discriminatory
basis, Christabel, along with some other suffragettes, simply
adopted a 'gender neutral' version of this perspective which,
of course, excluded most women (those who were not white,
Anglo-Saxon, Church of England and rich). At the ELF meeting
after her return from Paris, Sylvia said Emmeline and Christabel
'suggested that they [the WSPU] had a higher fighting standard,
but afterwards that was withdrawn'[89] – but it was, however, said
and remembered. Sylvia told the meeting the difference between
the two organisations was:

> we had more faith in what could be done by stirring up working women
> than was felt at [WSPU] headquarters, where they had most faith in
> what could be done for the vote by people of means + influence. In other
> words they said that they were working from the top down + we from
> the bottom up.[90]

The group, renamed the East London Federation of the
Suffragettes (ELFS), kept the suffragette colours with their
addition of red, and attained considerable influence in the area.
By the summer of 1914 there were five branches: in Bow and
Bromley, Poplar, Canning Town, South Hackney, and South
West Ham. From May 1914 they rented a hall and adjoining
house on Old Ford Road; the house becoming the new home for
Sylvia, Norah Smyth and the Paynes, and the newly christened
'Women's Hall', the ELFS headquarters, enabled more ambitious
plans: 'to organize a lending library, a choir, lectures, concerts
... The place became a hive of activity and the first house of

call for everyone in distress.'[91] They organised a Christmas
Savings Club and a 'Junior Suffragettes Club' for young women
between 14 and 18 years old. The increasing scope of initiatives
suggests a growing organisation. Further evidence of the way
in which the organisation grew can be seen in the way it used
its new newspaper.

The Woman's Dreadnought, launched in March 1914 with
Sylvia as its editor, is an extraordinary testament to her self-confidence in light of the fact she had never edited a newspaper before
and was continually in and out of prison. Even a policeman
arresting her in May 1914 asked 'how I found time for it'.[92]
Nevertheless, she wrote the vast majority of its articles and
ensured it appeared every week. The first edition read like a direct
riposte to the WSPU. It carried an uncompromising celebration
of the ELFS's history and political approach, and discussed
women's trade unions, while in another article Sylvia tackled
the moral panic around venereal diseases and prostitution.
Christabel's sensationalist book, *The Great Scourge*, had only
recently been published on the same subject, claiming the vast
majority of men used prostitutes and engaged in promiscuous
sex, thus concluding the 'true reason' men opposed votes for
women was their indulgence in 'sexual vice'.[93] She claimed 75–80
per cent of men had gonorrhoea before marriage, still more had
syphilis, and then there were the men who contracted venereal
diseases after marriage. Once again, women were cast as the
victims in WSPU propaganda, both as prostitutes and wives,
although it was wives Christabel was chiefly concerned with:
they were cast as 'the innocent' at risk of being made sterile, after
infection by their lascivious husbands, resulting in an apocalyptic
finale of 'Race Suicide!'[94] Sylvia, by contrast, started not from
the interests of 'the race' but from the life experience of the
prostitute: 'Medical knowledge can no more save them from the
life they are leading, than can the preaching of religious people
who tell them that their souls will go to hell; their minds, bodies,
and hearts are there already.'[95]

While Christabel blamed the sexual behaviour of almost every
man in the country (the book called for 'Votes for Women and
Chastity for Men'[96]), Sylvia did not even mention men who

used prostitutes, blaming instead the male establishment who, regardless of their individual behaviour, presided over the starvation wages of many women workers which made prostitution a systemic problem.

It seems Christabel's words in Paris were the target of Sylvia's article containing an impassioned defence of struggle from below:

> Some people tell us that it is neither specially important that working women should agitate for the Vote, nor specially important that they should have it. They forget that comparatively, the leisured comfortably situated women are but a little group, and the working-women a multitude.
>
> Some people say that the lives of working-women are too hard and their education too small for them to become a powerful force in winning the Vote, many though they are. Such people have forgotten their history. What sort of women were those women who marched to Versailles?
>
> Those Suffragists who say that it is the duty of the richer and more fortunate women to win the Vote, and that their poorer sisters need not feel themselves called upon to aid in the struggle appear, in using such arguments, to forget that it is the Vote for which we are fighting. The essential principle of the vote is that each one of us shall have a share of power to help himself or herself and us all. It is in direct opposition to the idea that some few, who are more favoured, shall help and teach and patronize the others.[97]

The paper was originally to be free but, due to their inability to cover costs, they charged a halfpenny in the first four days, and then distributed the remainder door-to-door around the East End.[98] They began by printing 20,000 copies a week and, although there were no collated figures, the paper's weekly reports show individual members sold hundreds each week. The journalists were ELFS activists who 'knew what to ask and how to win the confidence' of those they interviewed about housing and working conditions which, Sylvia recalled, 'produced far truer accounts than any Fleet Street journalist'.[99] Sylvia's emphasis on emancipation from below informed the paper's aim to amplify the voices of working-class women:

It was my earnest desire that it should be a medium through which
working women, however unlettered, might express themselves, and
find their interests defended ... I wanted the paper to be as far as possible
written from life; no dry arguments, but a vivid presentment of things as
they are, arguing always from the particular, with all its human features,
to the general principle.[100]

One measure of the newspaper's success was in its profile
amongst women who were taking action in the ferment of
the ongoing Great Unrest. The *Dreadnought* was only a few
weeks into publication when in nearby Millwall around 1,000
women and 600 men walked out of Morton's preserves and tea
packing factory in protest at women being replaced by young
girls on lower rates of pay. The strikers were combative and
lively, organising pickets and demonstrations; press photographs
showed them smiling and laughing and in one instance dancing
the tango in the streets. Florence Buchan, herself a jam factory
worker in Silvertown until she was sacked for suffragette
activities, interviewed them several times for the *Dreadnought*.
They told her the foreman had locked them in to stop them
striking and was given 'a good thrashing' when the male
workers found out; the women concluded 'there are too many
bosses'.[101] The ELFS were evidently respected by the strikers
as Miss Paterson, the Poplar ELFS organiser, addressed one
of their outdoor meetings, ELFS member Annie Lake spoke at
their meeting in Trafalgar Square, and some strikers attended
the ELFS Limehouse branch.[102] When the women at Pink's
jam factory struck again in 1914 Florence Buchan was there
to interview them and expose the management's harshness,
reporting 'Mr. Leonard Pink said at a coffee stall that he would
see the whole of Bermondsey weep before he would give in
to them.'[103] Some ELFS members were themselves integral to
strike action, like Annie Lake who organised a successful strike
at Johnnie Walker's bottling factory.[104] In June 1914 a strike
broke out at Bach's Asbestos Works in Bow where some of the
young workers were members of the ELFS's Junior Suffragettes
Club including 15-year-old Rose Pengelly, who was expected to
wash the boss's laundry and peel his potatoes, in addition to the

physically demanding factory work. One of the strike leaders, she was christened 'Sylvia' by her fellow workers – an indication of the esteem in which Sylvia was held by these local workers.[105] Two of the women workers agreed to speak at an upcoming ELFS meeting; the *Dreadnought* carried their story, putting a photograph of the strikers on its front page, and the strikers asked Sylvia to be their treasurer. The practical support the ELFS provided produced political gains – the girls in the asbestos factory were said to be 'enthusiastic about Votes for Women'.[106]

The Women's Hall became a centre for industrial unrest: 'Strikes, especially of women, and some of them only lasting a few days, were breaking out on all sides of us. All day our hall was often requisitioned for strike meetings; we were appealed to for speakers and help in every sort of way.'[107] The great reserve of energy and combativity in the Great Unrest that was untapped by the WSPU invigorated the suffrage struggle in the East End.

They also made efforts to engage politically with women working in the home who were more isolated. ELFS activists would choose a street, knock on every door and ask the women about their lives and what they thought about the vote. They argued with those who disagreed and invited all to ELFS meetings. The responses, recorded in the *Dreadnought*, exposed how difficult the women's lives were – one woman told Melvina Walker that when they could not make their husbands' wages go far enough 'then they start on you. It's a hard life.' Another 'did not think life was worth living, but must put up with it for the sake of the children.'[108] The ELFS's methods showed a broad conception of how oppression operated within the working class, which they refused to confine to the workplace. They tried to adapt the industrial weapon of strike action to help empower women in the home, by suggesting a rent strike for women's suffrage which would also force the issue of poor housing and profiteering landlords.[109] Although this plan did not come to fruition, it was powerfully employed by working-class women in the First World War.

The ELFS was even confident enough to attempt to force the furiously anti-women's suffrage Prime Minister, Asquith, to receive an ELFS deputation. While WSPU members had to rely

upon their leadership's judgement of which Bills to support –
which had themselves been drawn up by MPs – the ELFS asserted
control over the measure they would propose to Asquith by
voting on it at mass meetings across the East End. They voted
on three options: to leave the terms up to the government while
reserving the ELFS's right to criticise; votes on the same terms
as men; or votes for every woman over 21. The third option,
the most absolute and democratic, was at every meeting the
unanimous choice.[110] The mass meetings also chose who would
be on the deputation, which gave the audience a sense of a stake
in the outcome. When the Prime Minister refused to meet the
deputation, Sylvia tried again to fuse the collective methods that
had gone into defining the deputation with ultra-individualistic
militancy, declaring that she would, on her next re-arrest, hunger
and thirst strike and not stop after release from prison until
Asquith agreed to receive the deputation. She was now so weak
from frequent imprisonments she had to be carried on a stretcher,
and it was as she was being carried on an ELFS demonstration of
thousands from the East End to Westminster, on 10 June, that she
was arrested, starting the battle of wills with the Prime Minister.

Released on the 18th of June and unable to stand or sit without
feeling faint, she insisted that she and other ELFS comrades were
driven to Parliament where she continued the strike, lying by
Cromwell's statue. George Lansbury, the journalist Nevinson,
and leftwing MPs Wedgwood and Hardie (with whom Sylvia was
rebuilding a friendship) stood with the women and then went
to inform Asquith what was happening. The once intransigent
Asquith backed down. Outside Parliament there was jubilation
as supporters declared 'We are winning!'[111]

The deputation consisted of six women: Mrs Ford, a jam
factory worker since the age of eleven, whose husband was
too sick to work; Mrs Payne, the shoemaker Sylvia lived with;
Mrs Savoy, a brush maker since the age of ten whose husband
insisted she call herself Mrs Hughes for the day because he
did not want his name in the papers; Mrs Bird, the wife of a
transport worker with six children; Mrs Julia Scurr, a member
of the Poplar Board of Guardians who had been involved in the
women's unemployed marches from the East End in 1905; and

Mrs Daisy Parsons, a worker in a cigarette factory. Sylvia did not go – she had got what she wanted, for the working women to 'speak for themselves'.[112] They refused to accept the way in which the vote had always been granted – gradually, and with the richest first. Instead, they asserted that the vote was of greater importance to working-class women. Mrs Savoy made the point most dramatically, shoving one of her brushes in front of the alarmed Prime Minister and his officials who 'started nervously, as though they feared that the brush might be a bomb', and stating that her role as a worker defined her right to vote, while also getting some revenge on her husband: 'I do not like having to work 14 hours a day without having a voice on it, and I think when a woman works 14 hours a day she has a right to a vote, as my husband has, and he does not hardly work at all.'[113]

They outlined the wide-ranging social questions that they needed the vote to address. Mrs Scurr described women's low pay, the suicide rate of married women who could not make ends meet, the fact that working women's husbands died younger than other men, the fact that poorer women could not afford divorce, and the link between poverty, women's inferior social status, and prostitution. Mrs Bird spoke about the East End's poor housing, Mrs Ford related the sexual harassment she and fellow workers had experienced at work, the pressure to submit to it to keep their jobs, and the potential consequences of getting pregnant in which all the shame fell on the woman and not the man. She said that factories needed reforms in areas 'men do not really know anything about'. Mrs Parsons talked about the superior treatment male workers in the cigarette factory received in comparison to the women, while Mrs Payne spoke of the injustice that, as a woman, she had had no right to a say in how her mentally disabled daughter had been treated for her condition, telling the Prime Minister: 'when you make laws, such as this Mental Deficiency Bill, it is all very well to make them; but unless you have had dealings with the mentaly [sic] deficient people you do not know what they really need'.[114]

The speeches made by each woman demonstrated that for them the campaign for the vote was a campaign to transform every aspect of their lives. It was in response to this deputation that a change was noted in Asquith's language. While patronisingly telling the women how 'very difficult and complex' the problems they had raised were, he also recognised 'if the change has to come, we must face it boldly, and make it thorough going and democratic in its basis' in an 'unrestricted form'.[115] The Prime Minister who had been implacably opposed to votes for women was now discussing details of a Franchise Bill. His claimed support for an 'unrestricted' franchise suggests he was contemplating women voting on the same terms as men, which was more than was conceded after the First World War when women got the vote on a restricted basis. Despite all the WSPU's insistence on the greater strength, influence and intelligence of richer women, Asquith had been forced to negotiate by working-class women from the East End.

4

Resisting the War

THE GREAT BETRAYAL

On 1 August 1914 Sylvia Pankhurst wrote: 'All sorts of reasons that sound glorious and patriotic are invariably put forward in support of a declaration of war; but it is practically certain that every war of modern times has been fought with the purely materialistic object of forwarding the schemes and protecting the interests of powerful and wealthy financiers.'[1] Three days later, Britain, allied with France and Russia, declared war on Germany as years of tensions between imperial rivalries suddenly tipped over into armed conflict. On the day Britain declared war Sylvia was in Dublin, where she had gone to report for the *Dreadnought* about how British soldiers had shot at a jeering crowd, most of whom were children, killing three people and injuring many more.[2] Her presence in Ireland underlined her opposition to workers being divided by nation, race or gender, believing that workers had a common interest in uniting against the powerful. As soon as the First World War was declared, therefore, Sylvia was opposed to it, seeing that workers would be encouraged to fight each other for the material gain of their rulers.

The leaders of the women's and labour movements were pledged to oppose war. In 1913 the International Woman Suffrage Alliance (IWSA) stressed anti-militarism as a principle of the suffrage movement.[3] The Second International, the body to which socialist and social democratic parties, including Britain's Labour Party, were affiliated, vowed to organise general strikes to bring Europe to a halt in the event of war being declared. On the 2nd of August 1914 Britain's labour organisations organised an antiwar demonstration in Trafalgar Square.

But these expressions of internationalism in peacetime could not be read as indications that the parties involved totally rejected nationalist or imperialist ideas. It was only when war was declared that commitments to internationalism were really tested. A forewarning was provided when a planned meeting called by the suffragist NUWSS, and supported by the IWSA, happened to fall on the day Britain declared war. Some suffragists wanted to cancel the meeting, and the original resolutions were re-written so that they now called upon governments 'not yet involved' to work for a peaceful settlement, while the other called on women to 'offer their services to their country'.[4]

Some sections of the labour and women's movement became militantly prowar, including Ben Tillett and Will Thorne, veterans of New Unionism – both of whom had spoken at the August antiwar demonstration. Thorne even became Lieutenant-Colonel of the West Ham Volunteer Force.[5] Emmeline and Christabel vociferously supported the war, and suspended militancy and *The Suffragette*, which later reappeared in 1915 under the patriotic title *Britannia*. Virulently anti-German, in June 1915 they worked with the government to organise a women's 'Right to Serve' demonstration. Some WSPU members felt this to be a terrible betrayal, but in fact the position the leaders took was entirely consistent with the political trajectory of an organisation that had sought a Conservative government, sympathised with the Ulster Loyalists, and explicitly rejected the involvement of working-class women. NUWSS leader Mrs Fawcett also supported the war; in 1915 she condemned calls for peace as 'almost treachery'.[6]

Others were seduced into joining the war effort by the lure of 'influence' over government policy. Mary Macarthur of the National Federation of Women Workers, Marion Phillips of the Women's Labour League, and Margaret Bondfield – all of whom had expressed opposition to war before it started – joined the government-run Central Committee for the Employment of Women (CCEW) to give women temporary war work. Though the ILP opposed the war, as well as prominent Labour figures such as Keir Hardie and George Lansbury, the majority of the Labour leadership did not, and in 1915 Labour's Arthur

Henderson joined the wartime Coalition Cabinet. The co-option of Labour leaders soon changed their perspective. The prospect of industrial militancy looked very different when viewed from the window of a government office, and the government found it far more effective to have labour figures argue against unrest. Indeed, in March 1915 it was Henderson who arranged the Treasury Agreement in which trade union leaders agreed to abandon hard-won safeguards including the right to strike.

DEVELOPING A STRATEGY FOR THE EAST END

The co-option of the majority of labour and suffrage organisations into the war effort highlights the radicalism of Sylvia's opposition to the war from the very start. However, this same opposition also threatened to distance her from some of the people she had campaigned alongside for the past two years. Melvina Walker later described how the warmongers preyed on the poor in the East End, whipping up a patriotic hysteria:

> When War was declared, everybody who was 'anybody' in Poplar threw himself or herself into the job of recruiting. I happen to live in the East India Dock Road, two doors from the Recruiting Office. A better spot for that office was ... the parade ground of the unemployed ...
>
> Down came three or four 'buses filled with soldiers, and bands playing 'It's a Long Way to Tipperary,' 'Rule Britannia' and other such songs to stir up the people. Each 'bus displayed a white banner inscribed: 'Roll Up Boys, A Free Ride to Berlin.'
>
> Hundreds of men and women gathered round. Every man who walked up the steps to 'sign on' was treated as a hero; cheers were continually rising.[7]

Even at home Sylvia found Norah Smyth and Jessie Payne believed the war really was about defending Belgium and not, as Sylvia argued, 'fought for material gains'.[8] However, there were also members who supported Sylvia's view. Melvina Walker opposed the war from the outset, as did Elsie Taylor and Elsie Lagsding, whose brother became a Conscientious Objector, while Jessie Stephen left the WSPU over its espousal of patriotism and joined the ELFS instead.[9] Unlike the WSPU, ELFS policy was not proclaimed from above, but decided democratically, which now presented Sylvia with the problem of how to continue working with a group of campaigners whose views on the war differed so sharply, and how to develop a strategy around which all members could unite without compromising her own antiwar principles. At a special meeting two days after the British government committed the country to war Sylvia outlined three strategies:

1. To go on as if nothing had happened
2. To try to make things better for those suffering through the war
3. To make [political] capital out of the situation.[10]

Significantly, none of these strategies required any members to adopt an explicitly antiwar stance. Indeed, Sylvia told the meeting that 'we could not say much against the war at present as so many people have relations in it that they will not listen yet'.[11] The meeting decided on a combination of the three approaches Sylvia had put forward. Unlike the main suffrage organisations the ELFS decided to continue campaigning for the vote, linking the way war was high-handedly declared by politicians without recourse to public opinion to the undemocratic nature of a state that denied women the vote.[12] The ELFS decided to help improve conditions for ordinary people and assert the ELFS's political priorities by trying to get their members onto local committees and launching campaigns against attempts to shift the cost of the war onto the poor. As the price of food had already increased Mrs Bird and Miss Paterson suggested that 'we do our shopping for food at ordinary prices & if it is refused get others to back us and take the food'.[13] Sylvia later recalled that some women successfully put this into practice, as shopkeepers were afraid that calling the police would provoke a riot.[14]

    The ELFS swiftly formed a list of five demands which the organisation could unite and campaign around. The first called on the government to take control of the food supply 'in order that all may feed or starve together, without regard to wealth or social position', and that working-class women be consulted on the price and distribution of food. The second called for government committees to provide work for men and women at the rates set by the trade unions, with 'women to be paid at equal rates with men for equal work'. The third called for the moratorium that applied to debts over £5 to be extended to those below, as these were the debts incurred by the poor and least able to pay. The fourth called for committees dealing with food prices, employment and relief to include working-class women. The fifth demand was for votes for women.[15] Again these demands did not commit the members to explicitly denouncing the war, but they did demand that the war should not translate into increased suffering and exploitation for working-class men and women. In 1915, in an East End deputation to the Chancellor of the Exchequer, Reginald McKenna, Sylvia demanded that the government tax the rich and nationalise industry to fund the war instead of forcing workers into extreme poverty. When McKenna responded that 'rich people would not submit', Sylvia asked 'Would they prefer to submit, or to give up the War?'[16] The demand that the rich pay for the war they were so enthusiastic about had an underlying antiwar logic, as Sylvia put it at an ELFS general meeting: 'If we can make employers lose instead of making profits we would bring the war to an end.'[17] In September 1915 the *Woman's Dreadnought* exposed the lie that all were making equal sacrifices on a front page titled 'War Time Economics' with two contrasting photographs – the first, titled 'Ours', showed East End babies, the second, titled 'Theirs', showed members of Britain's upper class in dinner jackets at an opulent ball.[18]

The *Dreadnought*, however, did carry explicitly antiwar arguments. One of the most striking was a very early antiwar article titled 'working women and the war' by Melvina Walker. Written shortly after the first outbreak of anti-German rioting in the East End, when two German butchers shops were looted in Bow's Devons Road and Old Ford Road,[19] she argued that workers regardless of nationality had far more in common with each other than they did with the ruling class of their own countries by evoking the solidarity of German workers with the London dockers:

> How strange! British transport workers – trade union men – are called upon to shoot down German transport workers, and it is not so very long ago, in the time of our industrial war – I mean the great Dock Strike – when we were fighting the large ship owners, we received with joy the news that these same men had sent us £5,000 to help us in our fight for better conditions. We said we would never forget their kindness, let us keep our word by treating all those German workers who are left behind in our midst with civility.[20]

Sylvia later wrote an article condemning anti-German rioting in the aftermath of the sinking of the passenger ship the *Lusitania* by German U-boats, in which she told of the suffering of one of their Poplar members who, because her husband was German, had been a victim of the violence.[21] There was therefore nothing populist about the ELFS's appeal to class anger against the war, it was informed by a genuine internationalism that was unafraid to confront difficult arguments within the community it sought to appeal to.

RADICAL WELFARE

The disruption caused by the outbreak of war was particularly devastating in the already impoverished East End. That so many women called into the ELFS's Women's Hall for help was, as the ELFS proudly related, testament to the respect the organisation had in the community: 'It was intensely gratifying to realize that so many women felt that the Suffragettes were their friends.'[22] The ELFS set up a Distress Bureau to help the numerous individuals now coming through the door. Some women faced destitution after losing their employment and many women did not know how to apply for the separation allowance which was supposed to compensate for the loss of the wages of a husband or son who had joined the army. The authorities frequently lost applicants' forms and legal documents, and often the amounts awarded were wrong. In one particularly cruel case, the £7 granted to a soldier's widow was put into a bank rather than handed to her directly and when her child fell ill and she asked for the money she was informed by a lady from the Soldiers and Sailors Families Association (SSFA) that they had decided to take £5 from it and put it in the War Loan. Sylvia later commented archly that 'Patriotism was fashionable, and patriotism at other people's expense most fashionable of all.'[23]

Then there were cases of soldiers not receiving the correct compensation money after being wounded at the Front.[24] Sylvia regularly won improvements for the cases she took up and the ELFS began to act 'as a Trade Union or a family solicitor might have done'.[25] At the beginning of 1915 she extended the reach of this work by forming a League of Rights for Soldiers' and Sailors' Wives and Relatives, in which Lansbury's daughter-in-law Minnie Lansbury worked closely with Sylvia. Sylvia and Norah Smyth sacrificed a great deal to help their neighbours: 'Often I was constrained to take the food from our table to give to starving people, sometimes the blankets from our beds.'[26] Smyth lent money to people who could never repay her, while Sylvia worked through the night twice a week to keep up with the workload.

Sylvia was reluctant to set up welfare services herself for fear this would transform their organisation – which sought to empower women to fight for better conditions themselves – into a charity which provided better conditions *for* them: 'organised relief, even the kindliest and most understanding, might introduce some savour of patronage or condescension, and mar our affectionate comradeship, in which we were all equals'.[27] The distribution of free milk for malnourished babies, which Sylvia set up at the Women's Hall within a week of the outbreak of war, was therefore supposed to be temporary. But they were soon helping over 200 babies a day, and new milk and distress bureaus were set up in the ELFS centres in Poplar, Bromley and Canning Town. Each scheme suggested the necessity of another. These centres soon offered baby weighing; Sylvia hired a nurse to attend the Women's Hall every afternoon, and a doctor once a week, so that mothers could get help for their sick babies. Similar

clinics were then established in five other centres across the East
End.[28] Less than a month after the outbreak of war, Sylvia set
up a 'Cost Price Restaurant' – 'the name should be a slogan
against profiteering, and would carry no stigma of charity'.[29]
Again, the first restaurant was set up in the Women's Hall, and
others followed at the other ELFS centres. A two-course meal
was obtained by buying cheap tickets, although these were given
away free to those that could not afford them, with every care
taken to prevent anyone knowing who had bought and who had
been given tickets. As with the other schemes, Sylvia's plan was
to go beyond simply providing relief, in this case by collectivising
the labour usually imposed on women individually of cooking
family meals: 'Communal restaurants, supplying first-rate food
at cost price, were in line with our hope of emancipating the
mother from the too multifarious and often hugely conflicting
labours of the home.'[30]

Not everyone, however, remembered the food as exactly
'first-rate'. Sylvia persuaded Elsie Lagsding, who had trained as
a cook, to work at the Cost Price Restaurant on Railway Street

'The name should be a slogan against profiteering': the first Cost Price Restaurant at
the Women's Hall in Bow. Sylvia is third from the left on the far table.

in Poplar. Unable to afford meat, the menu was limited and even the cook was unsure of the ingredients: 'It was mostly offal that we had – we had to – I don't know what it was. It was called offal, I know that.'[31] Sylvia also directly employed local women on work to help others, starting with making maternity clothes for those who could not afford them.[32] This scheme required arrangements for the care of the workers' children during working hours. The ELFS rented another shop, and another scheme, a nursery, was established. Again, Sylvia would push the project beyond providing expediencies, and imbue it with an idealistic scheme to transform peoples' lives by employing the Women's Freedom League suffragette Muriel Matters to run the nursery along Montessori lines. Likewise, she wanted to make the work the ELFS provided more conducive to 'developing personal initiative and craft-skill' in the workforce.[33] To this end, she established a toy-making business and persuaded Amy Browning, her old friend from art school, to teach drawing and painting to those workers who wanted to improve their skills. Sylvia was overjoyed seeing the realisation of her early dreams of the role art could play – 'its happy cultural influence upon girls and women starved of beauty and opportunity' – poignantly celebrating their developing artistic creativity that she no longer had time for herself.[34] By January 1915, the ELFS could report that it was employing, in addition to its organising and secretarial staff, '59 regular indoor workers on relief work of one kind or another, all but five of whom are on full time, and also a varying number of outworkers'.[35] Sylvia insisted upon paying no less than the minimum wage that men received in the district, feeling that 'to pay a woman less, and call it charity, was to connive at sweating'.[36]

INDIVIDUAL AND COLLECTIVE RESISTANCE TO WAR

After the introduction of military conscription in 1916 many ILP members made individual stands against the war by refusing to fight, declaring themselves Conscientious Objectors (COs).

The ELFS supported COs and men on the run from the army: after the introduction of conscription one member in Bow hid her husband and brother-in-law until the end of the war, while Elsie Taylor delivered food parcels to a man known as 'Fred' who hid in a hole in the ground he dug in Epping Forest and sometimes stayed at Old Ford Road with Sylvia, Norah Smyth and the Paynes – a measure of how significantly Norah and Mrs Payne's positions on the war had altered since August 1914.[37] The *Dreadnought* reported the sufferings of the imprisoned COs and carried important exposés about the way in which they were being deported to the Front to be placed under army jurisdiction where they could be shot.[38] However, Sylvia resigned from the Council Against Conscription when it decided not to lobby MPs going to vote on the conscription Bill.[39] Sylvia's approach was far more extrovert, reflecting her view that the vast majority of people could be persuaded to oppose the war which was being waged for the benefit of the wealthy few and at the expense of everyone else. While they admired the personal courage of those who adopted individual stands against the war, the ELFS did not make such actions a condition of membership or a central focus of their organisation, understanding that to prioritise a moral individual stand could prove a barrier to the involvement of those in war work.

From the outset the ELFS recognised the potential of workers directly involved in the war to strike back powerfully against it. Their roots in the local community enabled them to understand that the decision to join the army was not necessarily motivated by support for the war: long before conscription was officially introduced, they identified economic conscription at work. On a deputation to Will Thorne, the MP for West Ham, ELFS member Charlotte Drake said of the spiralling cost of food: 'what it amounts to is that they are going to starve the men into joining the Army'.[40] This was confirmed by a local soldier who in December 1914 told the *Dreadnought* that when asked why they joined the army, soldiers replied 'because we were starving'.[41] The *Dreadnought*'s refusal to underestimate class tensions within war work enabled it to appeal to some soldiers. One soldier, a 'Poplar Boy' serving in France, wrote in September 1915 to the paper: 'I now have the pleasure of writing to you and your comrades to tell you how much I appreciate your paper, which the wife sends me every week. I might also tell you all the boys in the trenches where we are read it.'[42]

Despite intense efforts by the authorities to suppress all information about the mutiny in the British army at the notorious army camp at Étaples in France in late September 1917, the *Dreadnought* was able to report it on the front page because a soldier wrote in: 'The men out here are fed up with the whole b___y lot. About four weeks ago about 10,000 men had a big racket in Etaples, and they cleared the place from one end to the other, and when the General asked what was wrong, they said they wanted the war stopped. That was never in the papers.'[43]

The ELFS adopted a similar approach to women war workers. When the government introduced a National Register to record the details of everyone between the ages of 15 and 65, which laid the basis for introducing conscription, Sylvia and Norah Smyth decided not to cooperate and did not sign. However, the Federation did not make a shibboleth of refusal to sign, Sylvia understanding that

> I was surrounded by masses of poor women who had taken war work, soldiers' clothes and equipment, munitions, whatever came, as the sole means of keeping them and theirs from starvation. Inevitably they passed to war work as peace employment failed. For these women the fight against sweating must be maintained.[44]

Therefore, instead of demanding an individual stance, the Federation organised a collective campaign that women in war work *could* be involved in, by calling a demonstration on 'Registration Sunday', 15 August 1915, around concrete political and economic demands: 'No register without safeguards! No compulsion! Equal pay for men and women! Down with sweating! Wages must rise with prices! Down with high prices and profits! Votes for women to protect our homes and wages!'[45]

COMMUNITY-BASED RESISTANCE TO WAR

One of Sylvia's biographers argues that the Federation's energies, which they focused on organising welfare schemes and deputations to Parliament, would have been better redirected around organising among factory workers to campaign themselves for demands such as equal pay.[46] An explanation of Sylvia's focus requires a comparison between the ELFS's position in London's East End with those areas of the country which did see strike action in the early years of the war.

In February 1915 the pay agreement for the engineering workers in the munitions factories on the Clyde expired. The employers' new offer in no way reflected the huge leap in rent and food prices so the engineers, in defiance of their union leadership, took unofficial strike action and elected their own strike committee directly from the factory shopfloor. A second strike on the Clyde broke out in spring 1916 over the victimisation of a shop steward investigating the conditions of new workers they were afraid were 'diluting' (or undercutting) existing workers' jobs. A strike of South Wales coalminers broke out in July 1915 when their wage agreement expired, and they won all their demands after five days.[47] Sylvia fully supported both disputes. Due to her friendship with Hardie, whose constituency was Merthyr Tydfil in South Wales, she had connections with socialists there and regularly spent weekends on speaking tours of the colliery towns.[48] She happened to be there when the strike started and was able to speak to the strikers offering her support. She was also among the speakers invited to Glasgow to speak in support of the action on the Clyde. Why then was urging strike action amongst women workers not the focus of Sylvia's activity in London? For a start, the strikes in Glasgow and South Wales benefited enormously from the influence and implantation of active socialists. In Glasgow there were leading socialists working in the engineering factories who dominated the leadership of the rank-and-file organisations, meanwhile outside the factories the activist John Maclean had carried on very popular Marxist educational classes for workers.

In Wales Sylvia was impressed by the depth of the strike leaders self-education in socialist ideas:

> These leaders were omnivorous readers of Blue Books, company prospectuses, and theoretical works on Economics. Marxist devotees of the Central Labour College in London and its classes throughout the valleys, they had nevertheless a special South Wales cult of their own, and some of them even talked of 'marching on London,' to take it for the proletariat when the hour of social revolution struck.[49]

The ELFS had nothing like the strength or influence of these socialist organisations. Although they did not keep membership figures, they did note in July 1915 that they had less than 1,000 members,[50] and there is no evidence that they had any members in the munitions factories that employed large numbers of women from 1915. The Federation's focus on women workers created additional complexities. The huge loss of women's jobs at the outbreak of war probably saw the Federation lose most of the influence it had in prewar workplaces, and when the asbestos factory opposite the Women's Hall threw its employees out of work, including the Junior Suffragette and strike leader Rose Pengelly, the ELFS lost what had looked like its strongest base.[51]

Further, women munitions workers faced additional pressures. The employers quickly identified the potential offered by these new, unorganised workers who, as women, were used to low pay. Many were forced to work an excessive, and often illegal, number of hours (92 hour weeks were reported), in dangerous working conditions with poisonous chemicals, for which they were paid less than male workers.[52] This gave rise to resentment among male workers who feared the women were undercutting their jobs, forcing them to face military recruitment during the war and unemployment after it, which resulted in the intimidation of and hostility towards the women by some of the male workers.[53] This was exacerbated by the chauvinism of the 'craft' unions such as the Amalgamated Society of Engineers, which organised munitions workers, who refused to 'dilute' their membership by admitting women, thereby making it harder for women workers to fight alongside the men for the same conditions. Therefore,

work was perhaps not the place that many women felt most
confident campaigning in.

In focusing on community rather than workplace agitation,
the ELFS concentrated on the most fruitful area of women's
resistance in the first years of the war. In Glasgow, where
landlords had been rapidly increasing rent since the start of the
war, news spread in March 1915 that a woman whose husband
had been wounded in action and who also had two sons at the
Front was facing eviction after falling into rent arrears of less
than £1.[54] This news, which seemed to epitomise the way in
which those fighting the war were being exploited at home, saw
hundreds turn out to prevent the serving of an eviction notice
and then the declaration of a rent strike across Glasgow. The
strike was militant and dominated by women. Mary Barbour
from Govan organised flying pickets to resist the bailiffs which
became dubbed 'Mrs Barbour's Army'.[55] Sylvia remembered
that 'women kept watch all night on the common stair of the
barrack dwellings, their neighbours heartening them with tea in
their cold vigil. The men who came to serve the ejectment orders
were greeted with volleys of flour.'[56] The landlords taking the
matter to court only inflamed the situation, men in the shipyards
struck in protest and an angry demonstration converged on the
court. Under this pressure the landlords dropped the action and
the government passed an Act which restricted rent throughout
the war. Although the movement in Glasgow was exceptional
in its intensity, it showed how community struggles could give
strength to industrial struggles, and that popular movements
could force significant concessions even in wartime.

The ELFS's activities in the early years of the war suggest a
similar appreciation of the role that community resistance could
play. The three marches on Parliament it organised between July
and September 1915 took up industrial demands but expressed
them outside of the workplace. Sylvia recalled that the thousands
who joined the July 1915 march against sweated labour were
composed of 'the sweated workers come to plead their own
cause'.[57] By the end of 1915 Sylvia had made contact with at
least one munitions worker in Croydon whose letter, in response
to Sylvia's questions, exposed the poor wages and commented

'already the women are coming to me to say they cannot live on them'.[58] By 1916, presumably through contacts like these, Sylvia was able to expose the dangerous conditions munitions workers faced that were being denied, covered-up or down-played by their employers; two front-page headlines read 'Dope Poisoning: Dangers to Women Aircraft Workers' and 'T.N.T. The Latest Industrial Poison'.[59]

Further, the deputations to government did not take place in isolation from the local community. For example, in early 1917 a local meeting elected representatives to a deputation over food prices; these then reported back at another meeting.[60] These deputations were not organised on the assumption that the ministers would be persuaded to see things from the women's point of view; Sylvia had at least since 1912 explicitly rejected politicians patronisingly operating 'on behalf' of the people. But the deputations did aim to persuade the politicians that it was in their interests to do what the women suggested, which is rather different. Sometimes this came in the form of a threat: in their deputation to Runciman, the President of the Board of Trade, at which they demanded that the government control food prices, Melvina Walker banged the table warning 'Something must be done for us, or we shall have to take the food!'[61] Moreover, they were also attempting to demonstrate to the government that there would be serious consequences if the ELFS's fourth demand – representation of working-class women on committees for food prices, employment and relief – was not realised. This particularly challenged the legitimacy of those figures in the labour movement who the government had co-opted early in the war to accurately represent working-class interests.

After their deputation to Mary Macarthur, in which they unsuccessfully attempted to urge her to get rid of the sweated wage in the Queen Mary Workrooms, Mrs Drake's report in the *Dreadnought* commented bitterly on the 'splendid, furnished apartment' Macarthur received them in after her lunch, on which Drake remarked, 'and I do not suppose the lunch cost at the rate of the 10s. a week that she seems to think is enough for women who are thrown out of employment through this terrible war'.[62] Thus, even when the deputations did not change the government's position, the report-backs at meetings and in the *Dreadnought* enabled the Federation to argue the importance of more direct working-class representation by exposing the inadequacy of their supposed representatives.

It is difficult to quantify exactly how successful the ELFS were in their efforts, but it is unlikely to be a coincidence that in October 1916 the *Dreadnought* was reporting a strike of hundreds of workers at Schneider's Clothing Factory, which supplied army clothing, in the East End's Whitechapel. The strikers won all their demands, one of which stated that if any worker was dismissed the case could be referred to a committee of the workers' elected representatives whose decision would be final, which was reminiscent of the Federation's demand for direct working-class representation. This demand was then taken up by workers in another army clothing factory in Whitechapel.[63]

WORKERS' SUFFRAGE

The ELFS had developed a more radical interpretation of democracy: beyond the individual right to vote they demanded guaranteed representation in government on the basis of their class. Although their prewar demand of a vote for every woman over 21 was implicitly a demand for adult suffrage (the government would hardly enfranchise all working-class women *before* all working-class men), in January 1916 they voted to explicitly support 'human suffrage' – a vote for all men and women.[64] Meanwhile those societies that had suspended their campaign for the vote and joined the war effort had developed a more conservative assessment of what the movement could fight for. When the question of electoral reform appeared again in the government's agenda, a number of suffrage societies met to discuss a united demand. Sylvia proposed human suffrage and was supported by Emmeline Pethick-Lawrence and some figures who had left the NUWSS,[65] but the NUWSS refused to support it and one delegate later claimed 'Miss Pankhurst, to my amazement and disgust, seeing the sense of the meeting was going against her, began to round on us as a lot of "comfortable middle class women".'[66]

Once again, Sylvia found herself fearing that the middle-class women, who had stopped fighting for the vote, would dictate the terms on which the vote would be granted and see those who had continued fighting left out. In March 1916 the ELFS changed its name to the Workers Suffrage Federation (WSF) to reflect the particular importance it attached to the working-class vote.

WAR AND IMPERIALISM

Sylvia's radicalism also created tensions in the Women's International League (WIL), which emerged out of an international conference of women who wanted to see an end to the war, in the Hague in April 1915. (In Britain, 180 women, including Sylvia, had wanted to attend the meeting, but the government refused Sylvia a passport and then stopped shipping from crossing the North Sea.) Sylvia was on the executive of the British branch, but the WIL voted against the WSF's proposal that they call themselves the Women's International Peace League, and rejected foreign women members and even wives of 'enemy aliens'.[67] Much of the leadership were women who had felt forced to leave the nationalist NUWSS in order to participate in the WIL, and although they were unhappy at the war they had accepted the notion of serving the nation in wartime and were unable to fully break with looking out for the interests of 'their' state and therefore rejected the notion of campaigning for peace on any terms. Sylvia, however, was moving in a very different direction; she spent the war reading 'Karl Marx, Kropotkin, William Godwin, William Morris – all those who attacked the ethics of present society at its base took on a deeper meaning', and developed an understanding of the war as driven by imperialism.[68] In an article asking 'What is a Pacifist?' she answered 'the true pacifist is a rebel against the present organisation of society'.[*][69]

---

[*]   The term 'pacifist' was a much broader term in the early twentieth century than it is now. It did not mean the absolute renunciation of all violence, but it did entail demanding an immediate end to war. (See 'Preface' in Wiltsher, *Most Dangerous Women*, p. xii.)

Sylvia later explained her turn towards explicit antiwar campaigning as a consequence of a personally traumatic experience. In September 1915 she was devastated by the news that Keir Hardie had died. She felt that 'the War had shattered him',[70] while George Bernard Shaw, the Fabian socialist, commented 'I do not see what Hardie could do but die' when 'the Labour Party he had so painfully dragged into existence – should snatch still more eagerly at the War to surrender those liberties and escape back into servility, crying: "You may trust your masters: they will treat you well." ... This was what broke the will to live in Keir Hardie.'[71]

Reflecting on Hardie caused Sylvia to dwell upon her own campaigning focus in the first year of the war. She explained her dilemma as an internal dialogue: 'though I had spoken against the War, the greater part of my struggle had been waged for economic conditions. "Oh yes, I know this is a capitalist war; if capitalism were ended, wars would be no more; yet the politics of this War, in their callous wickedness; these you have not sufficiently exposed".'[72] But though Hardie had been opposed to the war, he was primarily opposed to it from a moral standpoint; that he was unable to galvanise collective opposition was reflected in Sylvia and Shaw's depiction of him as a broken, isolated individual. Sylvia's opposition to the war was motivated both by her commitment to the ethical socialism represented by Hardie, but also by a more scientific socialism which saw the war as fundamentally opposed to the interests of the vast majority of people. She was therefore able to identify 'economic conditions' where inequalities were intensified in wartime, which people could unite around and challenge. Though personally horrified by the war, Sylvia therefore never felt as isolated as Hardie did, and although she felt his influence as her emphasis changed, she did not in fact change her approach of working towards collective, popular resistance. Indeed, her move towards campaigning for peace coincided with a shift in public opinion against the war. The enthusiasm for a war that would be 'over by Christmas' 1914 evaporated as it turned into a bloody war of attrition in which a single day could bring tens of thousands of casualties. The drive in 1915 towards conscription, introduced in

1916, reflected the fact that not enough men were volunteering to continue the war, while the intensified hardships on the home front, which Sylvia had identified as the basis of opposition, were translating into disillusionment in the war.[73] The *Dreadnought* reflected this changing consciousness; in one instance in March 1916 it reported the reaction of striking women munitions workers in Newcastle who were told to go back to work for the sake of the soldiers: 'A girl waved her hand and said: "Don't mention the soldiers. England at 2½d. an hour isn't worth fighting for!"'[74]

The discontent was reflected in the increased numbers of strikes that broke out in 1915 and 1916; and then at Easter 1916 an uprising in Dublin against British rule was brutally crushed, and the leaders executed in prison. Sylvia was most affected by the execution of Connolly, whom she had spoken alongside in 1913, and whose socialism she felt was the greatest loss to the movement for Irish freedom 'because his rebellion struck deeper than mere nationalism'.[75]

Sylvia's shift in emphasis, then, largely developed out of her own reading in this period and her identifying the opportunity that a change in popular consciousness provided for more explicit antiwar campaigning. In December 1916 she launched a peace campaign, holding demonstrations at the East India Dock Gates and Victoria Park. The police made arrests claiming there was disorder, but Sylvia and other WSF members argued that they had largely sympathetic audiences and the disorder was exaggerated to give the impression the country remained overwhelmingly prowar and as a pretext to remove antiwar campaigners from the streets. Sylvia would later remember: 'Peace, and the popular government of the world to end this capitalist system of ruthless materialism, stood out for me as the two great needs of the hour.'[76] This more explicitly socialist and anti-imperialist agitation would come to define her activity for the next few years.

The WSF's rejection of a 'national interest' from the very start of the war, and their insistence on the particular, but international, interest of the working class, enabled them to develop a defence of women's rights in wartime, which had been abandoned by other women's organisations, and a more complete antiwar position than the international organisations working towards, but not for, peace. No wonder that the WIL chair Helena Swanwick found Sylvia 'a very provoking colleague, owing to her habit of going her own separate way, even after she had joined others in hammering out an agreed way ... like one of the hoops in "Alice's" game of croquet, Sylvia had wandered off to another part of the field'.[77]

Then, in March 1917, everything would change again. Elsie Lagsding found out while she was sitting in a socialist meeting – Norah Smyth came 'rushing in and she said "the revolution's started, it's started". They all sat and gaped at her, they thought she'd gone mad.'[78]

5

Sylvia's Communism

THE FEBRUARY REVOLUTION

The spark that set Russia ablaze came from 'the most oppressed and downtrodden part of the proletariat'.[1] On the 23rd of February 1917,* International Women's Day, women textile workers in St Petersburg went on strike. They sent delegations into the metal factories and called out the men. On the streets the starving women in the huge bread-queues joined them and they converged on the town council demanding bread. The protests quickly gained momentum; the next day the slogan was no longer 'bread' but 'down with autocracy' and 'down with the war'.[2] The years of pent-up bitterness at the slaughter on the Eastern Front, dire poverty, scarcity and endless queues, political repression and the oppressive regimes in the factories, now exploded onto the streets. The strikes and demonstrations grew increasingly militant, defying the violence used against them until the troops mutinied and joined the revolution. The Tsar, the most reactionary ruler in Europe, was overthrown and replaced with a Provisional Government.

The British government and the rightwing, prowar newspaper *The Times* declared their support for the revolution. Before the February Revolution they were in the embarrassing situation of claiming to fight a war for freedom while allied with the autocratic Russian Tsar. Their support for the February Revolution was based on the wishful thinking that the revolution was over. Now with the Liberal Prince Lvov at the head of the

---

* Before 1918 Russia used the Julian calendar and not the Gregorian calendar used in Western Europe. Thus, 23 February in Russia was 8 March in Western Europe. When writing about pre-1918 events in Russia I use the Julian calendar.

Provisional Government they hoped for a far more intensive prosecution of the war from Russia. But the Provisional Government's commitment to the war was diametrically opposed to the demands of the revolution and the revolution was very far from over.

SYLVIA DIAGNOSES DUAL POWER

The February Revolution saw the revival of workers' councils, or *soviets*, that had first been created in the ferment of the 1905 Russian Revolution. Made up of delegates elected by workers from their workplaces and soldiers from their battalions, the soviets reflected the mood of the working class and conscripted peasants. In the Petrograd soviet, 1,200 delegates were soon meeting every day.[3] The soviets spread rapidly: by June 1917 there were 519 across Russia.[4] There were therefore two powers produced by the February Revolution: the popular, democratic soviets and the Provisional Government led by a prince. It was this tension between the ideas of those who had made the revolution, who were organised in the soviets, and those congealed around the Provisional Government, who wanted only superficial political and not social change, that made dual power such a volatile condition.

One of the first people in Britain to identify the revolutionary potential in the Russian situation was Sylvia Pankhurst. Immediately after hearing about the February Revolution Sylvia wrote in the *Dreadnought* editorial: 'At present there are virtually two Governments in Russia – the Provisional Government appointed by the Duma and the Council of Labour Deputies* which is responsible to the elected representatives of the workers and the soldiers.'[5] In this article, titled 'Whose Russian Revolution?', she saw that the nature of the revolution

---

* The Duma was the Russian Parliament. By 'Council of Labour Deputies' Sylvia is referring to workers' councils (soviets).

and which class it belonged to had not been decisively answered in February, and would only be answered by future struggles.

THE WSF'S CONTACT WITH RUSSIA

Sylvia's perceptive analysis was partly due to her contact with Russian socialists. One was Peter Petroff, a veteran of the 1905 revolution who lived in exile in Britain and wrote for the paper *Nashe Slovo* (Our World), produced in Paris by another Russian revolutionary exile, Leon Trotsky.[6] As early as May 1915 Petroff spoke on the topic of Russian women for a WSF meeting in their Women's Hall. Petroff was close to Glasgow revolutionary John Maclean and the Glasgow British Socialist Party (BSP) branch had members from Latvia who were also exiles of the 1905 revolution. Almost all Sylvia's references to the soviets of 1905 consist of detailed information about the involvement of the Latvian Social Democratic Workers' Party in their local soviet, which indicates that she had contact with the Glasgow Russians.[7] Her most direct source was George Chicherin, another *Nashe Slovo* writer, who gave her the newspaper published in Switzerland by Lenin, the leader of the Russian revolutionary Bolshevik Party.

Meanwhile, the WSF's antiwar agitation was pulling them into contact with the East End's Jewish community, many of whom had fled anti-Semitic pogroms in the Russian Empire. This community, forced into sweated labour in the East End slums, was regarded with racist hostility by the British authorities who suspected them of having little interest in fighting a war for the British state, especially for a British state allied with the country they had fled in fear of their lives. Early contact came in 1916 when a Jewish family in Whitechapel allowed Sylvia to publish the letters their son, a soldier in the British army, sent them before he was court martialed and shot for desertion. The letters suggest he was suffering from shellshock and Sylvia published them in a pamphlet, *Execution of an East London Boy*, which called for an end to executions at the Front.[8]

After the Conscription Act came into force, Sylvia attended the Bethnal Green military tribunal, which judged the claims for military exemption, where she witnessed institutional anti-Semitism: 'Jews were treated even more relentlessly than other applicants; the destruction of their small businesses seemed to give real satisfaction to the Tribunal.'[9] She came into more direct contact with the Jewish community after the announcement in autumn 1916 that Russians in Britain would have to choose between fighting in the British or Russian army.[10] When in January 1917 the British government intercepted a neutral ship bound for America to arrest Russian Jewish passengers and deport them back to Russia for military service, a protest meeting was organised in the East End. The meeting at the Premierland Cinema on Stepney's Commercial Road was in the main attended by the local Jewish community, half the platform addressing the audience of over 2,000 people in Yiddish. Such was the esteem in which Sylvia was held that she was among the speakers.[11] Throughout the year before the February Revolution Sylvia was thus campaigning alongside a community with personal experience of Russia and a vested interest in the revolution effecting fundamental social change, particularly an end to racial oppression and to participation in the war, which they feared they might be pressed into at any moment. This was powerfully demonstrated when the news of the revolution reached East London. On two consecutive days two huge celebratory meetings were held. The first, organised in Mile End by the Committee of Delegates of Russian Groups, was 'an indescribable, unforgettable demonstration of enthusiasm, unbounded joy and revolutionary feeling. Over 7,000 persons were present, and many thousands were unable to get in and had to go away. During the whole meeting again and again outbursts of boundless enthusiasm filled the immense hall with unending applause and shouts.'[12] The second, held just up the road in Whitechapel by the Foreign Jews Protection Committee, was also completely packed and had to turn people away,

whilst those inside sang Russian revolutionary songs, which thrilled the heart with their majestic melancholy. The gangways were thronged, the light was dimmed by the close-packed crowds standing against the windows in the gallery. The audience was a swaying mass of humanity that easily broke forth into cheers and cries of enthusiasm for the coming freedom or groans of hatred and contempt for the tyranny that is overthrown.[13]

Symbolic of the newly constructed alliances was the fact that a local suffragette and an Irishwoman were among the platform speakers. Both audiences longed for the revolution to develop further and stop the war – cheers turned to icy silence when the chair of the Whitechapel meeting spoke in favour of the war, while the Mile End meeting, where Russian sailors appeared on the platform, explicitly allied itself with the soviets: 'The meeting also expressed its conviction that all those who have at heart the cause of the workers and of all the labouring masses in Russia must rally around the Council of Workers and Soldiers' Delegates for the successful achievement of the work of the Revolution in the Republic of Russia.'[14] The WSF themselves had a Russian member, Mrs Bouvier, who attempted to raise the argument for deepening the revolution amongst Russians based in Britain. In May 1917 she went to speak to a celebration of the revolution meeting in Liverpool intending to address a hundred Russian sailors based in the port, but the Russian Consulate forbade them from attending.[15]

Sylvia's emphasis on socialism from below predisposed her to support the soviets, but her revolutionary Russian contacts and links with a politicised local Jewish community undoubtedly aided her in declaring her support so swiftly and made her stance so distinct from other widespread celebrations of the revolution.

THE RUSSIAN REVOLUTION AND THE BRITISH LEFT

The WSF grasped the revolutionary and antiwar potential of the February Revolution more swiftly and completely than any other organisation on the British left. This can partly be attributed to the organisation's small size and its acceptance of Sylvia's leadership. However it was also because it was already engaged in explicitly antiwar agitation from the end of 1916. In late February 1917 WSF member Melvina Walker was arrested and fined after a meeting in Hyde Park where she 'asked why should we send mothers' sons to murder other mothers' sons? "Our class in Germany was just as good as we are. What we want is peace ... *It is up to us workers to end the War*.'[16] The WSF was therefore able to seize on the revolution as evidence that the working class could stop the war without falling for the ever-elusive solution of a 'negotiated peace'. At a meeting in Brighton to celebrate the Russian Revolution, attended by 1,600 people, Sylvia exposed the false argument that strikes in the arms industry would endanger the troops at the Front, explaining 'The truth is that the more guns you send out the more men will be killed.'[17] In March 1917 the WSF disrupted 'National Service Week' recruitment rallies. In Poplar the local press reported that, 'beginning by meek interjections, Suffragettes, soon revealing that they were in force grew gradually more noisy' until they were 'ejected with some vigour'.[18] The WSF increasingly changed its focus from specifically working-class women's issues to the issues of the working class more generally. In June 1917 the *Woman's Dreadnought* was re-named the *Workers' Dreadnought*, and in 1918 the Workers' Suffrage Federation became the Workers' Socialist Federation.

In this period the WSF worked closely with the BSP, particularly those members who saw the relevance of the February Revolution to revolutionary, antiwar propaganda in Britain. However, the BSP as a whole did not take the outright revolutionary position of the WSF, many preferring individual moral objection to the war. It is significant that Sylvia first approached the BSP with the idea of fusing their organisations in the summer of 1918, after 'hearing that almost the whole of the B.S.P. Executive would be affected by the raising of the conscription age',[19] presumably feeling that this would force them into extrovert antiwar campaigning.

Other sections of the British left seized cynically on the revolution in desperate attempts to restore their credibility with Britain's angry and war-weary workers. The same Labour politicians who had enthusiastically supported the war effort, joined the government that had allied with Tsarist Russia, torn up workers' rights and civil liberties and allowed big business to make massive profits out of the war while the poor suffered intense shortages, were now declaring themselves revolutionaries. Attending the March 1917 Labour Party Conference Sylvia was astounded to hear MP Will Thorne, the Lieutenant-Colonel of West Ham, move the resolution to congratulate the Russians: 'he said that he supposed he had been chosen to perform the office because, "I am a revolutionary and a red-flagger"'.[20]

Those in the Labour Party who were genuinely enthusiastic about the February Revolution and those who had cynically decided to champion it in the hope of downplaying the radical repercussions in Britain converged in an ambiguous project in the summer of 1917. After organising a huge meeting in the Albert Hall to celebrate the revolution, Lansbury called an organising meeting of his newly formed Anglo-Russian Alliance in an office on the Strand. He invited Sylvia, who was bemused by their grandiose plans: 'We met thus, just a few of us, in a small room. The business was disclosed to us by the Alliance as no less a project than the formation of the Workers' and Soldiers' council of Great Britain, which was to take control of the British Revolution.'[21] There was such a yawning disparity between the politics of the people present, including Labour politicians Ramsay Macdonald and Philip Snowden, and their revolutionary rhetoric, that Sylvia was stunned into silence:

I contributed [sic], I think, not a word to the discussion; I listened in complete amazement to sentiments so revolutionary from such unexpected quarter, and wondered what the world could be coming to when, some of those present, who had been shocked by the mild militancy of the Suffragettes, should be discussing such a tremendous step.[22]

This meeting called a national conference in Leeds in June 1917 attended by 11,051 delegates from across the labour movement. Sylvia observed that, compared to the platform speakers, the audience was further to the left, more working-class, and included a much greater proportion of women. The speakers diverted the enthusiasm of the audience towards motions of support for the revolution abroad. The only practical motion called for the establishment of Councils of Workmen's and Soldiers' Delegates, but the revolutionary language masked the moderate intentions. Only the name had been borrowed from the Russians. These English councils intended to resist attacks on civil liberties and workers' rights, give 'special attention' to women's position in industry, support the trade unions, oppose profiteering and 'concern themselves with' military pensions and soldiers' rights. These rather vague commitments were similar to the kind of campaigns Sylvia had launched in the first year of the war, and there was no intention that these councils should, like the Russian councils, pose an alternative form of government. Sylvia noted this contradiction, writing 'It foreshadows revolution: yet it concerns itself with matters of detail which are obviously part and parcel of the present system.'[23] She was reluctant to get involved and refused to be nominated as a delegate to the resulting Councils, but her name was put forward in a postal vote without her knowledge and she was duly elected. There was no intention that the Councils be campaigning organisations. Only a few meetings were ever held, and Sylvia turned up late one day to find the Council had disbanded. She had written to the Secretary immediately before asking that her ideas for activity be discussed, which she believed 'had administered the death blow ... the shock of a concrete policy coming before it had perhaps killed the Council'.[24]

All this revolutionary posturing was exposed when a second Russian Revolution broke out in October 1917. After the revolutionary socialist Bolsheviks won majorities in Russia's largest soviets they called for a second revolution to overthrow the capitalist, warmongering Provisional Government and replace it instead with a soviet government. The ambiguities of dual power were swept away as workers, peasants and soldiers seized control of their own futures and began to effect massive social changes. One of the first things the new Bolshevik government did was to pull Russia out of the First World War. In Britain, almost all those who had declared their admiration for the February Revolution were vitriolic about October because, as Sylvia identified at the time, it was qualitatively different from all previous revolutions: 'the outstanding fact [is] that the Russian Revolution is a Socialist Revolution, and that its aims and ideals are incompatible with those of capitalism'.[25]

Reactions to the October Revolution proved which forces were truly revolutionary and which would ultimately side with the continuing rule of capitalism. At the 1918 Labour Party Conference the invited guest was Kerensky, the Russian Prime Minister overthrown by the October Revolution, who made a speech calling for military intervention in Russia. Sylvia found her motion calling on Labour to withdraw from the government ruled out of order and her speech attacking Britain's foreign policy shouted down by the Chairman.[26]

Sylvia herself wholeheartedly supported the October Revolution which represented for her the realisation of working-class self-emancipation.

'HANDS OFF RUSSIA': DEFENDING THE REVOLUTION

The Great Powers were agreed: the Bolshevik Revolution must be crushed. A huge propaganda campaign was launched demonising the Bolsheviks to prepare public opinion for military intervention. In 1918 one of the WSF's Russian contacts, the violinist Edward Soermus, proposed that Sylvia establish a Russian Society to disseminate accurate information about the Russian Revolution.[27] The WSF initiated the People's Russian Information Bureau (PRIB), in July 1918, winning the support of socialist and labour organisations. Its committee included Sylvia, representing the WSF, alongside representatives from the largely Scottish-based Socialist Labour Party (SLP), the BSP, the National Union of Railwaymen, Shapurji Saklatvala for the ILP,* and W.F. Watson from the rank-and-file London Workers' Committee. The committee included Russians, but to protect them the PRIB kept their names secret. The wisdom of this was

---

* In 1922 Saklatvala became one of the Communist Party's first MPs and Britain's third Indian MP.

underlined the night before the first PRIB meeting when Soermus
was arrested and subsequently deported to Russia.[28] The PRIB
printed pamphlets from foreign journalists in Russia sympathetic
to the revolution, such as Philips Price, and from the leading
Bolsheviks. As many of these texts risked prosecution under the
Defence of the Realm Act (DORA), a restrictive censorship act
introduced during the war, they had to be printed secretly. This
included one of the PRIB's most important pamphlets, Lenin's
Appeal to the Toiling Masses, which called on workers to strike
in the event of military intervention in Russia. Sylvia remembered
that they 'posted batches of it to comrades we judged willing to
distribute it. The recipients did not know whence these parcels
had come. They were posted sometimes in London, sometimes
in the provinces.'[29] WSF member Harry Pollitt, of the River
Thames Shop Stewards Movement, later recalled:

> Sylvia Pankhurst kept us continuously supplied with copies of Lenin's
> *Appeal to the Toiling Masses* ... My landlady in Poplar one day expressed
> surprise that my mattress seemed to vary in size from day to day, and 'that
> I must be a rough sleeper, as it was so bumpy.' She little knew that inside
> the mattress we kept our copies of Lenin's *Appeal*, and each day took a
> supply to distribute amongst the workers in the docks and shipyards.[30]

The underground activities of the PRIB attracted the unwelcome
attention of Special Branch, the section of police who gathered
intelligence on so-called subversives. In 1918 W.F. Watson became
a target of police spies, who could always rely upon finding
him in licensed premises. On two occasions police suggested
that they pay him for information about the revolutionary left,
and although at first he refused after a few drinks he changed
his mind. When this was exposed Watson was hopelessly
compromised, although he claimed he thought he was protecting
the movement by feeding the police useless information. His
account of what took place indicates Special Branch's particular
interest in the PRIB; one policeman said 'he would like to know
where this People's Russian Information Bureau was established
and where they got the information from. He also wanted to
know where all the Bolshevik literature came from.'[31] He also

confronted Watson with a copy of Lenin's *Appeal* demanding to know where it was printed. The answer was rather closer that they perhaps realised. Sylvia later recalled that the door to the PRIB offices was a heavy sliding one that used to fall out of place, which sometimes meant 'the help of two or three burly policemen had to be requisitioned to test their strength on it'.[32]

The WSF was well-placed to agitate against British intervention as it was from the East End docks that munitions were loaded onto ships bound for Poland, from where attacks on Russia were launched. In January 1919 Sylvia was elected to the committee of the Hands Off Russia campaign at the founding conference called by the BSP, the SLP and the International Workers of the World (IWW), and soon 'Hands Off Russia' became the slogan of the anti-intervention movement. Melvina Walker took the lead. Pollitt remembered

> how indefatigably the late comrade, Mrs. Walker of Poplar, used to work for the 'Hands Off Russia' movement. She toiled like a Trojan. If on a shopping morning you went down Chrisp Street, Poplar, you could rely upon seeing Mrs. Walker talking to groups of women, telling them about Russia, how we must help them, and asking them to tell their husbands 'to keep their eyes skinned to see that no munitions went to help those who were trying to crush the Russian Revolution'.[33]

Women therefore played the leading role in arguing for industrial action. It was a hard argument to win. The bosses were paying the dockers extra to load the munitions, and when Pollitt, the leading activist, was sacked for refusing to load munitions for Poland no one at work took action to defend him. But there were signs of growing discontent. The night Pollitt was sacked a workmate told him 'What are you worrying about, Harry? It'll all come right in the end', and a few weeks later the rope attaching the ship to the munitions barges mysteriously snapped and the barges sank in the middle of the North Sea. The WSF intensified its campaign and 'Mrs. Walker worked herself to a standstill.'[34] Then, on the 10th of May 1920, when the dockers were ordered to load guns for Poland onto a ship called the *Jolly George*, they refused to touch them. The action quickly spread,

'The coalies heard a great commotion amongst the dockers and
asked the cause of the trouble. When they learnt it, they refused
to coal the ship.'[35] The dockers went to their union officials Fred
Thompson and Ernest Bevin who said that they would support
strike action. The *Jolly George* strike was a significant victory
which helped lead to the establishment of nationwide anti-
interventionist councils of action and the British government's
abandonment of the idea of intervening directly in Russia.

1919: THE MISSED OPPORTUNITY

With the end of the First World War in November 1918 came
a gathering storm of hatred against the rulers who had sent
millions to die in the horror of industrialised warfare, and
watched the people suffer and mourn while big business made
huge profits from the killing industry. The Easter Rising in Ireland
and the Russian Revolutions were followed by mutinies in the
French army and the German navy which brought an end to the
slaughter. In November 1918 a German revolution overthrew
the Kaiser and declared a republic. In Britain the last years of the
war saw mounting industrial unrest. In 1918 there were nearly
6 million working days lost through strikes which were now
being waged even by groups the government least expected to
take militant action: in August 1918 women bus workers struck
for equal pay and a month later the police went on strike.[36] In
October 1918 Lord Burnham warned the head of Special Branch:
'We cannot hope to escape some sort of revolution ... and there
will be no passionate resistance from anybody.'[37]

The British government tried desperately to dissipate the anger
by offering reforms, including votes for women. Publicly they
claimed it was a 'reward' for women's patriotic war work, but
in fact it was precisely the young women who worked in the
munitions factories that were excluded from the vote as the
government decided to enfranchise women over the age of 30,
although men could vote from the age of 21. As urgent demands
for change always come from the young, granting the vote to

older women was less a reward for patriotism during the war than a bribe for patriotism *after* it.

The government were right to scramble for support. War-sick soldiers were horrified to discover that the British government planned to send thousands of them off to fight another war, this time against the Bolsheviks. In 1919 the discontent exploded into strikes and mutinies that shook the foundations of the British state. There was an average of over 100,000 people on strike for every working day of 1919.[38] On the 3rd of January 10,000 soldiers at Folkestone refused to be sent for service abroad. Thousands more mutinied in the following weeks, a Soldiers' Union was formed, and around 150 soldiers at Osterley Park took hold of army vehicles, drove into London and demonstrated outside Downing Street.[39] Mutinying sailors at Milford Haven raised the red flag on the *HMS Kilbride*. There was a wave of unofficial strikes in the mines, and in Scotland at the end of January thousands joined a strike in the engineering factories. Their demonstration in Glasgow was so brutally attacked by the police it became known as Bloody Friday. That night six tanks were sent to Glasgow and the strike leaders were arrested. In February there were strikes on the railway and the London tube; in April the Mersey dockers struck; in June 450,000 cotton workers struck for 18 days; July saw another miners' and rail strike. In August the police went on strike for the second time in two years. To quell the disorder a battleship and two destroyers were sent up the Mersey and troops were sent into Liverpool.

However, the different strands of discontent failed to come together. Profoundly influenced by syndicalism – which argues that the working class is won to revolutionary change through industrial action alone, and which therefore neglects the question of the development of political consciousness and action – the industrial rank-and-file movement in engineering excluded political aims from its strikes. Despite the fact that the strike leaders were antiwar they did not call a strike against the war through which they might have made common cause with the mutinying troops. Further, the different groups of workers had no centre from which to coordinate their action, so struggles across industry for a reduction in working hours never agreed upon a united demand, and the government negotiated separately with each group of workers leaving them divided and, therefore, weakened.[40]

The leaders of the unions and the Labour Party could not unite the movement as they did not want to see a movement powerful enough to challenge state power. Had there been a party whose every effort was directed towards a revolutionary challenge to state power it could have pointed out the value of united demands and coordinated action. In 1919 the Third International,* established by the Bolsheviks, urged far left organisations across Europe to do just that by forming communist parties. The WSF was the first organisation in Britain to call itself the Communist Party, adopting the name at its annual conference in June 1919. Nevertheless, a few days later it decided to suspend its use of the name pending the outcome of its unity discussions with the BSP, the SLP and the South Wales Socialist Society (SWSS), which now focused on uniting with a view to becoming a Communist Party.[41] However, the unity discussions soon divided over their approaches to Parliament and the Labour Party.

Sylvia had been infuriated at Labour Party conferences by Labour's evident loyalty to the nation-state and not to the revolutionary working-class movement. Moreover, the experience of the First World War had shown that social democratic parties had spectacularly failed to represent working-class interests as they supported the war effort and even joined the national governments conducting the slaughter of millions of working-class men in the trenches. In January 1919 the German social democratic government that took power after the German revolution sent the proto-fascist paramilitary Freikorps to crush

---

*   The Third (Communist) International was a revolutionary, international coordinating body and represented a conscious departure from the Second International to which social democratic parties, including the Labour Party, were affiliated and which had failed to organise resistance to the outbreak of war.

a working-class uprising in Berlin culminating in the murder of revolutionaries Rosa Luxemburg and Karl Liebknecht. Revolutionaries concluded that social democratic parties, committed to the reform of but not the overthrow of capitalism, were fundamentally unable to emancipate the working class, and Sylvia felt that communists should therefore refuse to be involved in any way with social democratic parties or parliamentary democracy. The WSF, alongside the SLP and SWSS, wanted the Communist Party to have no affiliation to Labour, but the BSP, which was itself affiliated to Labour, disagreed. The BSP and SLP were in favour of engaging in parliamentary elections, the WSF and SWSS were completely against this.

The quarrel quickly attracted Lenin's attention and in 1919 he conducted a debate with Sylvia in the Third International's publication, *Communist International*. He argued that although Sylvia's assessment that revolutionary change could not come through Parliament or the Labour Party was correct, this was not the view of most working-class people in Britain. The communists should not, therefore, separate themselves off from the majority of workers, instead communists should try to use Parliament as a platform from which to expose its inadequacy. However, Lenin stressed above all the urgency of forming a British Communist Party. Although he was in favour of revolutionaries participating in Parliament, he argued that this was 'now a partial, secondary question'[42] and that it was 'better to make a mistake than to delay the formation of a big workers' Communist Party in Britain out of all the trends and elements ... which sympathise with Bolshevism and sincerely support the Soviet Republic'.[43] He even went on to add that if British revolutionaries could not agree 'I should consider a good step forward to complete unity the immediate formation of *two* Communist Parties.'[44] But in 1919 Sylvia, like many of the others involved in the negotiations, believed compromising ideologically by forging a party with those whom she disagreed with was too high a price to pay. Moreover, the British Communists did not appreciate the importance of timing: there were two more years of arguing before the British Communist Party was founded,

by which time the potentially revolutionary moment of 1919
had long passed.

SOVIETS

For Sylvia, the most important thing about the Russian
Revolution was the creation of the soviets. This more direct form
of democracy, based in the working class, seemed to provide the
antidote to parliamentary democracy. Sylvia believed that the
mere existence of a superior alternative would automatically
bring about working-class disillusionment in reformism.
However, what had actually taken place in Russia and across
Europe proved this was not the case. In Russia reformists
dominated the soviets in the largest cities right up until the
autumn of 1917. The Bolsheviks' call for a second revolution
only became popular after the reformists massively discredited
themselves by allying with an extreme rightwing attempted
putsch while the Bolsheviks won widespread credibility for
organising resistance to the putsch. In Berlin in January 1919
the revolutionary Spartakist League, of which Luxemburg
was a leading member, argued that any attempt to set up a
revolutionary government would be fatally isolated by the fact
that the vast majority of the German working class were not
yet engaged in revolutionary struggles. The Spartakist League
was far too small to influence the direction of events, and the
attempted workers' government was crushed.[45] In Britain, talk
of establishing soviets at the Leeds Conference in May 1917
came to nothing because Labour politicians like Macdonald and
Lansbury dominated proceedings. In each case, the prospects
for the successful establishment of working-class government
depended on whether revolutionaries had the organisational
strength to influence developments.

However, Sylvia allowed her fetishisation of soviets to
obstruct her from uniting with others in a revolutionary party.
Her emphasis on the democratic forms of the future was so
total that it came at the expense of agitating in the present.
The detrimental effect was felt in the WSF; at one meeting Mrs

Pascoe said 'the workers could not understand about Russia', while Melvina Walker 'protested that the Dreadnought was too academic'.[46] Sylvia justified the changed emphasis on the basis that international revolutionary politics were of greater importance than local clamours for reform: 'publishing Soviet Government decrees, speeches and articles of Lenin and the rest[, and] news of the intervention [meant] we had less space to devote in our small paper to the woes of our people'.[47] In truth she was failing to link the problems of the East End to the revolutionary movement and ought to have been alarmed when such a staunch campaigner as Melvina Walker was one of those who felt they had got the balance wrong.

WOMEN AND THE RUSSIAN REVOLUTION

Revolution always sees those oppressed under the old regime throw themselves into the heart of the struggle for a new society, and the Russian Revolution, ignited by women workers in February 1917, was no different. The Bolsheviks were profoundly committed to achieving women's liberation. Addressing the First All-Russia Congress of Working Women in 1918, Lenin declared 'The experience of all liberation movements has shown that the success of a revolution depends on how much the women take part in it.'[48]

Social transformation followed rapidly after the October Revolution: all legislation discriminating against children born outside marriage was abolished; civil marriage replaced church marriage with equal rights for both partners and complete freedom to divorce; women gained the right to vote, equal pay and paid maternity leave; abortion was legalised and so was homosexuality. The Bolshevik government included Alexandra Kollontai, one of the foremost writers on women's liberation.

In Britain the attitude of suffragettes towards the October Revolution threw into sharp relief the divisions that had emerged in the prewar movement. The WSPU leadership were terrified by the social ferment in Russia. In the summer of 1917 Emmeline Pankhurst travelled to Russia to put pressure on the government to remain in the war. Whilst there she took the salute of the Women's Battalion of Death, a military unit formed by Kerensky to increase the moral pressure on men to keep fighting in the war. After the October Revolution Emmeline made campaigning against Bolshevism her main focus.

Many of those who saw the campaign for the vote as a campaign for radical social change, especially those who had split from the WSPU, were more inclined to support the revolution. As well as Sylvia and the WSF, Dora Montefiore, who left the WSPU to campaign for adult suffrage, Charlotte Despard, the leader of the Women's Freedom League, and the Glasgow suffragette Helen Crawfurd, supported the October Revolution and became early members of the British Communist Party.

Sylvia supported the October Revolution because it promised working-class emancipation. She saw women's liberation as an integral part of that goal, never losing her particular interest in the women's movement. When she went to Russia she extensively visited clinics, orphanages and houses for mothers and children, generally finding them inspirational, and was impressed by the new laws relating to women. She also began to envisage soviets expanding beyond workplaces to democratise spaces largely occupied by women so that delegates to soviets of the future 'shall be themselves workers, drawn ... from the bench, the mine, the desk, the kitchen, or the nursery'.[49] She also suggested that 'street soviets' be constructed to bring rent, housing and food under democratic control.[50]

SYLVIA AT THE HEART OF INTERNATIONAL DEBATES

In late 1917 Sylvia met an Italian revolutionary named Silvio Corio and the two fell in love. Born in 1877 in Turin, Corio had fled political persecution in Italy, moved to France, and after being expelled by the French government settled in London. A journalist and trained compositor he joined the exiled Italian anarchists living in London and continued to produce anarchist propaganda. His technical training was of enormous practical use to the PRIB and Sylvia also appreciated the change in atmosphere his presence brought: 'He imported a fresh humour and an insight which were enlivening.'[51] Having been the dominant political strategist in the WSF, Sylvia welcomed the chance to work alongside someone else who was politically experienced: 'It was delightfully stimulating to have someone to plan with whose knowledge of world socialist movements was older and wider than mine who had read all that mattered of socialist writings and manifestos.'[52]

However, not everyone was overjoyed at this new addition to the team. WSF members May O'Callaghan, Nellie Cressell and Elsie Lagsding disliked him, and although this was perhaps partly due to differing personalities, Norah Smyth's complaint that Sylvia was spending increasingly more time with Corio, who was printing in Fleet Street, and less time in the East End suggests that resentment of Corio was also connected to tensions within the WSF.[53] At the same time that some members felt that the *Dreadnought* was overly concerned with international developments at the expense of local issues, Corio's knowledge of Italian politics probably only exacerbated these tensions as Sylvia became more deeply involved with the debates in the European communist movement.

At the end of 1919 and the beginning of 1920 Sylvia made trips – clandestine since she had been denied a passport – to Italy, Germany and Holland. In Italy she attended the conference of the Italian Socialist Party (PSI) where she supported the 'abstentionist' faction, led by Amadeo Bordiga, which argued against any participation in reformist politics. Italy was in the midst of the *biennio rosso* (red years): workers were occupying their factories, peasants seizing land, and Sylvia was struck by the revolutionary enthusiasm of the conference festooned with red banners and punctuated with cries of 'Viva Lenin!' The *Dreadnought* also warned that the terrified Italian bourgeoisie were turning to the paramilitary *arditi* who planted a bomb in a PSI demonstration, which they reported resulted in the arrest of several *arditi* leaders including a 'Benito Missolini [*sic*]'.[54] Yet this seemed a marginal threat – for now.

The situation was very different in Germany, which Sylvia had to reach by walking across the Alps by night, finding shelter with

anyone who would agree to break the law by taking in someone
without a passport. In May 1919 the workers' government
established in Munich was violently crushed by the Freikorps,
ushering in a wave of repression. Arriving in Stuttgart late at
night, Sylvia found all the communist addresses had been raided
and her contacts had fled. The next day she walked to the home
of the longstanding revolutionary Clara Zetkin and the two
travelled to Frankfurt where they attended a secret conference
attended by communists, amongst whom was Paul Levi, the
leader of the German Communist Party, who was in hiding from
the post-Munich witch-hunt.

In January 1920 Sylvia deepened her association with the
abstentionist communists when she and Norah Smyth attended
a conference in Amsterdam organised by the Dutch Communist
Party who were fiercely opposed to any parliamentary activity.
Sylvia came home emboldened by the conference vote against
British Communists affiliating to the Labour Party.[55]

LEFTWING COMMUNISM: SYLVIA DEBATES WITH LENIN

Fearing that they would be outvoted in the approaching
Communist Unity Convention on the 1st of August 1920, the
WSF called its own conference in June attended by seven small
locally based left groups and a few supportive individuals.
They voted to call themselves the Communist Party (British
Section of the Third International) (CP(BSTI)) despite having
a claimed membership of only 150.[56] However, despite their
stated allegiance to the Third International, Lenin opposed this
breakaway from the unity negotiations and Sylvia's allegiance
to the abstentionist position. He encouraged Sylvia to attend
and discuss the question at the second Congress of the Third
International held in the summer of 1920 in Russia. Once again
denied a passport, she had to smuggle herself aboard ships to
get there and back.[57]

As well as Sylvia, there were the British revolutionary shop
stewards Willie Gallacher and J.T. Murphy, Rosmer from
France, Wijnkoop from the Netherlands, and Bordiga from

At the heart of the international Communist debates. Sylvia (on the right) next to Willie Gallacher (in the bow tie) at the Second Congress of the Third International in Moscow, 1920.

Italy, who all supported abstentionist positions. On arrival delegates were given a copy of Lenin's new pamphlet *'Left-Wing' Communism: An Infantile Disorder* which specifically criticised the arguments put forward by Sylvia and Gallacher. The ensuing debate grappled with how communists ought to act in Britain where social democracy had deep roots and the Labour Party commanded the allegiance of vast numbers of workers.

Sylvia argued that the only way the British communists could avoid building illusions in reformism was by refusing to engage with it: 'The Communist Party must keep its doctrine pure, and its independence of Reformism inviolate.'[58] She even maintained that parties which advocated reform were more dangerous than openly reactionary ones because 'The bourgeois social patriotic parties, whether they call themselves Labour or Socialist, are everywhere working against the Communist revolution, and they are more dangerous to it than the aggressive capitalist because the reforms they seek to introduce may keep the capitalist *regime* going for some time to come.'[59]

Lenin, by contrast, argued that to change workers' ideas 'propaganda and agitation are not enough. For this the masses

must have their own political experience.'[60] If the communists
were a small minority there was no reason why the masses would
take their word for it that Labour would ultimately defend
capitalism. The British working class needed to *experience* the
betrayal by Labour to be open to communist ideas. Therefore a
Labour government would *aid* the communists and not hinder
them as Sylvia argued. Lenin agreed that the Labour Party was
'led by reactionaries, and the worst kind of reactionaries at that,
who act quite in the spirit of the bourgeoisie. It is an organization
of the bourgeoisie, which exists to systematically dupe the
workers.'[61] However, the Labour membership and supporters
were precisely the workers that the communists wanted to
convince. Lenin therefore argued that the Communist Party
should apply to affiliate to Labour (but only on the condition of
maintaining their complete freedom of speech within the Labour
Party) in order to come into contact with those workers with
whom they could argue the case for revolutionary change in a
tangible, and not abstract, way:

> At present the British Communists very often find it hard to approach the
> masses and even to get a hearing from them. If I come out as a Communist
> and call for the workers to vote for Henderson against Lloyd George,
> they will certainly give me a hearing. And I will be able to explain in a
> popular manner not only why soviets are better than parliament and
> why the dictatorship of the proletariat is better than the dictatorship
> of Churchill (disguised by the signboard of bourgeois 'democracy'), but
> also that I want with my vote to support Henderson in the same way as
> the rope supports a hanged man – that the impending establishment of
> a government of Hendersons will prove that I am right, will bring the
> masses over to my side.[62]

If Labour refused to admit or expelled the communists then this
too could only help expose Labour in practice.

Lenin's position was overwhelmingly endorsed by the
conference (58 to 24 with two abstentions) which came as little
surprise since the leaders of the Russian Revolution naturally
commanded the greatest respect.[63] However, the Russians were
committed to winning over their British comrades; Murphy

remembered 'the Russians seemed to be incapable of exhaustion by discussion'.[64] Lenin continued to meet with them emphasising that the position on Labour was a tactic and not a principle; it ought not to be an excuse for stalling the creation of a Communist Party, but had to be tried in practice to bring communists into greater contact with the working class. Sylvia was impressed by this extrovert approach: 'He is for attacking every such difficulty, not for avoiding it: he is for dragging Communist controversy out into the market-place, not closeting it amongst selected circles of enthusiasts.'[65]

Sylvia, Gallacher and Murphy returned with a changed approach to unity. Although Sylvia was still personally committed to her abstentionist position she now agreed that there should be one Communist Party for which she was prepared to compromise considerably. On her return she called a CP(BSTI) conference in Manchester in September 1920 where she argued for and won the conference's full support for the decisions of the Third International conference in Moscow.[66] They approached the Communist Party of Great Britain (CPGB), which had been founded at the Unity Convention on 1 August 1920, for renewed unity negotiations.

THE *WORKERS' DREADNOUGHT*:
ANTI-RACISM AND CLASS STRUGGLE

East London was culturally and ethnically diverse: Stepney was home to a large Jewish community, in Poplar there were families of Irish descent, and Limehouse had a Chinese community. In the First World War, Sylvia had seen how racism was used to deflect anger away from the powerful by dividing working-class communities amongst themselves. This understanding of racism enabled the *Dreadnought* to stand up to the attacks on German shops in the first years of the war. As the war became increasingly unpopular the military tribunals and much of the local press made scapegoats of the Jewish community, denouncing them as traitors and 'shirkers'. In 1917 the police poured fuel onto the fire by conducting raids in East London, dragging Jews off the streets ostensibly to investigate whether they were evading military service. In an article titled 'A Pogrom in London', Sylvia denounced the raids as state-orchestrated anti-Semitism in which thousands of men, including those far too old or young for military service and those with papers proving military discharge, were dragged out of clubs and restaurants, beaten up and detained in dangerously overcrowded police cells.[67]

Sylvia was also among those who spoke at meetings in the International Club, a radical multicultural meeting place in Charlotte Street off the Tottenham Court Road. The Jamaican poet Claude McKay who frequented the club described the vibrant cultural mix:

> The International Club was full of excitement, with its dogmatists and doctrinaires of radical left ideas: Socialists, Communists, anarchists, syndicalists, one-big-unionists and trade unionists, soap-boxers, poetasters, scribblers, editors of little radical sheets which flourish in London. But foreigners formed the majority of the membership. The Jewish element was the largest. The Polish Jews and the Russian Jews were always intellectually at odds. The German Jews were aloof. There were also Czechs, Italians, and Irish nationalists, and rumors of spies.[68]

McKay himself was attracted to the *Dreadnought*'s uncompromising opposition to racism. During demobilisation at the end of the war, shipping bosses made black British workers bear the brunt of the job losses. Thousands of black workers were left suddenly unemployed; the government deliberately kept them unaware of the money they could claim on losing their jobs and the unions colluded in the discrimination.[69] In 1919, fear of unemployment as industry restructured, combined with officially sanctioned racism, sparked race riots in ports across Britain. Black men were killed, their lodgings burnt, and typically they were blamed by the press for the violence, particularly if they retaliated.[70] There were riots in the East End, and Sylvia later recalled 'returning home one evening down East India Dock Road, and I found the place thronged. I asked, "What is the matter?" and I was told, "They are stabbing coloured men."'

Some were killed that night, and for three nights the thing went on in Poplar.'[71]

In a combative article the *Dreadnought* argued that workers should organise together rather than turn against each other: 'Do you not think you would be better employed in getting conditions made right for yourself and your fellow workers than in stabbing a blackman [*sic*] [?]' It also encouraged its readers to identify with black people as fellow victims of British imperialism: 'Do you not know that the capitalists, and especially the British capitalists, have seized, by force of arms, the countries inhabited by black people and are ruling those countries and the black inhabitants for their own profit?'[72]

But much of the British left was imbued with racist attitudes. In 1920 Lansbury's *Daily Herald* published an article by E.D. Morel, a prominent critic of imperialism, which denounced France's postwar occupation of the German Ruhr valley as an act of imperialism. However, Morel did so by highlighting France's use of black troops who, he argued, were a special danger to white women whom they raped and infected with syphilis. The article's title 'BLACK SCOURGE IN EUROPE: Sexual Horror Let Loose by France on the Rhine' was particularly inflammatory. McKay was incensed by the article, on which he would later comment ironically: 'Maybe I was not civilized enough to understand why the sex of the black race should be put on exhibition to persuade the English people to decide which white gang should control the coal and iron of the Ruhr.'[73]

He sent a response to Lansbury who, after assuring McKay he personally was not racist, made his excuses and did not publish it. It is testament to the reputation of the *Dreadnought* that he chose to send it there.* Sylvia published the article which stated that rape was wrong whichever race committed it and that articles like Morel's would only inflame racial tensions.[74] Sylvia offered McKay a job on the paper and in doing so made

---

* McKay's autobiography gives the impression that it was through finding a place for this article that he first came across Sylvia Pankhurst and the *Dreadnought*, but this was not the case as the *Dreadnought* had published one of his articles, 'Socialism and the Negro', on its front page three months earlier.

history: she was the first British newspaper editor to employ a black reporter.[75] McKay later recalled the meeting where they discussed his new job: 'She said she wanted me to do some work for the *Workers' Dreadnought*. Perhaps I could dig up something along the London docks from the colored as well as the white seamen and write from a point of view which would be fresh and different.'[76] Sylvia had a natural instinct as an editor; McKay would produce some of the *Dreadnought*'s most explosive articles. In 1920 McKay commissioned an article by a young seafarer named Springhall urging communists to call on workers in the armed forces to refuse to be used as strike-breakers. The article, 'Discontent on the Lower Deck', was published on the *Dreadnought*'s front page under a pseudonym to protect the author. In the same edition was McKay's article (published under the pseudonym Leon Lopez) on the mainstream press's attempt to get unemployed dockers to direct their anger onto the Chinese. He finished by calling on the dockers to turn their anger on the wealthy:

> The dockers, instead of being unduly concerned about the presence of their coloured fellow men, who, like themselves, are the victims of Capitalism and Civilisation, should turn their attention to the huge stores of wealth along the water front. The country's riches are not in the West End, in the palatial houses of the suburbs; they are stored in the East End, and the jobless should lead the attack on the bastilles, the bonded warehouses along the docks to solve the question of unemployment.[77]

This was too much for the authorities who saw McKay's article as an incitement to loot the docks and were alarmed by the prospect of agitation in the navy which had been among the most militant sections of the unrest in 1919. The *Dreadnought* offices were raided and Sylvia, as the editor, was held responsible and charged under the DORA with 'an act calculated and likely to cause sedition amongst His Majesty's Forces, in the Navy, and among the civilian population'.[78]

Sylvia took full responsibility, refusing to give the authors' names to the authorities. She used her trial to call for the overthrow of capitalism: 'although I have been a Socialist all my life, I have tried to palliate this capitalist system ... but all my experience showed that it was useless trying to palliate an impossible system. This is a wrong system, and has got to be smashed. I would give my life to smash it.'[79] The Alderman sitting in judgement declared 'such ideas can only enter into perverted minds'.[80] Although sentenced to six months in the Second Division, Sylvia appealed and was allowed out on bail until after the New Year.

EXPULSION

In the meantime, in the project to form a united Communist Party, an argument was brewing over the status of the *Dreadnought*. While the unity talks between the CPGB and the CP(BSTI) were conducted in the run-up to a National Convention of the organisations on the 29th and 30th January 1921, the CP(BSTI) executive made every effort to distinguish itself from the *Dreadnought*, perhaps because they felt it might jeopardise their chances of joining the CPGB. The Third International insisted that all communist journals be under the control of the Party's Central Committee to ensure their accountability to the organisations they purported to represent. However, Sylvia made it clear that she saw the *Dreadnought*'s role as representing the views of an abstentionist faction within a newly united Communist Party.[81] On the 1st of January 1921 the CP(BSTI) executive went as far as passing a resolution to boycott the *Dreadnought*. While it was true that the existence of a communist publication dedicated to arguing a different perspective to that of the leadership would likely have been divisive, it was remarkably crass of the CP(BSTI) leadership, which had never made itself liable for the content or finances of the paper, to focus on the problematic nature of Sylvia's control of the publication just at the time she was facing six months in prison for having taken sole responsibility hitherto. The proposal to boycott the paper at this time was hardly an attempt to build bridges or seek compromise, indeed it seemed like a deliberate attempt to completely alienate Sylvia from the proceedings.

At the National Convention, the CP(BSTI) merged into the CPGB but Sylvia was unable to take part; on the 5th of January 1921 Sylvia's conviction was upheld and she was sent to Holloway prison for the last time. Too little had changed since her time as a suffragette and, as before, she publicised the poor conditions and humiliating treatment of prisoners on her release. But unlike before there was no mass movement protesting against her imprisonment and the Communist Party made no attempt to galvanise one. On her release in May 1921 she was greeted by East End friends but not the CPGB leadership. The welcome breakfast was described as a 'small, almost devotional party'.[82]

These experiences seemed to have hardened Sylvia's abstentionist opposition and she now saw all compromises made by revolutionaries as betrayals of principle. In Russia, the Bolshevik call for a second revolution in 1917 had been based on the understanding that there could be no such thing as 'socialism in one country'. Russia was not sufficiently industrially developed to support all its citizens in a comfortable standard of living and would therefore need more industrialised countries to have revolutions to enable Russia to have enough for all. However, since there were no other revolutions in Europe that brought the working class to power, the Russian communists were forced to introduce elements of capitalist business to maintain the country. A group in Russia called the Workers' Opposition opposed these compromises. The *Dreadnought* printed their statements and identified with its insistence that the compromise itself, rather than regrettable material circumstances, was the real problem – a perspective that complemented Sylvia's approach to British politics.

By 1921 the postwar rise in unemployment had become deeply entrenched. Workers were policed into obedience by the knowledge that they could easily be replaced by anyone from the growing numbers of unemployed. The working-class defiance of 1919 had turned to fear. Workers were now reluctant to take battles into their own hands and were looking to other forces to fight their battles for them. Such a battle took place in 1921 when the Labour-dominated Poplar Council went on a rates strike: collecting the rates only for local services and refusing to pay the additional rates for London-wide bodies, such as the Police or Asylum Boards, arguing that this hit poorer boroughs hardest and that there ought instead to be 'equalisation of the rates' with richer boroughs contributing more than the poorer ones.[83] The Poplar councillors were sent to prison and their stand for fairness inspired admiration across East London. Among those imprisoned were many who had worked alongside Sylvia in the past: Minnie Lansbury, Edgar Lansbury, Julia Scurr, Nellie Cressall and veteran socialist George Lansbury who was head of the council. Yet instead of welcoming the councillors' actions and trying to transform working-class support into self-confidence, Sylvia dismissed the councillors' efforts and told workers, who were reluctant to fight over anything, that their only hope was to fight for nothing less than full communism:

> End the system. That is the only message the Communists can give to the workers: end the system; set up Soviets of your own, and through them build up a new and better life for all.
>
> The Poplar Councillors in prison are doing what they can: they ask you to run forward a little step to capture a little post on the road; we ask you to keep your eyes fixed on the final goal; to make straight for it, and concentrate your energies not on palliatives, but on making your fellow workers into Communists.[84]

By this time there was no prospect of a harmonious relationship between Sylvia and the CPGB. The leadership seemed determined to drive her out and she now wanted her paper to represent the Workers' Opposition and the abstentionist split from the German Communist Party which had stormed out of the Third International Congress in 1920. In September 1921 Sylvia was summoned to a meeting where she refused to hand over control of the *Dreadnought* and was immediately expelled from the Communist Party.

6
Anti-Fascism, Women and Democracy

In September 1920 the *biennio rosso* in Italy reached a climax when 400,000 engineering workers occupied hundreds of engineering factories after bosses at the Alfa Romeo factory in Milan locked out their workforce. Errico Malatesta, the Italian anarchist and friend of Silvio Corio, warned revolutionaries 'if we let this favourable moment pass, we shall pay later with tears of blood for the fear we have installed in the bourgeoisie'.[1] The truth of this was soon tragically realised. The leadership of the trade unions and the Italian Socialist Party (PSI), for all their radical slogans, had no strategy to spread the action and prepare a challenge to the state. Instead the occupations ended in a compromise with the bosses and Italy's ruling class looked around for a way to ensure that this threat would never happen again. Over the next two years they increasingly turned to the paramilitary terroristic group, who called themselves fascists, led by Benito Mussolini. The fascists received 74 per cent of their funding from banks, insurance companies, industrialists and business – the Italian ruling class desperate to ensure their own stability.[2] The fascists terrorised the enemies of the Italian ruling class. They attacked peasants occupying land in the countryside while in the towns they beat up and killed socialists and destroyed hundreds of centres used by the left and labour movement. This was the kind of control Italian big business wanted. The police colluded in the rise of fascist violence and the state bestowed official legitimacy on them; the Prime Minister included fascists on his 1921 electoral slate.

Despite all this support, the fascists' rise to power was not inevitable. Popular resistance organised around the *arditi del popolo* saw the fascists driven back from towns they had intended to terrorise. But the resistance was weakened by the lack of unity on the left. The reformist leadership of the PSI who hoped that the state would act to stop the fascists signed a peace pact with Mussolini in August 1921 in which they renounced involvement in the *arditi del popolo*. The Italian Communist Party (PCI), formed in January 1921, was led by Bordiga, Sylvia's old ally, whose sectarian insistence on not cooperating with those with illusions in Parliament meant that on too many occasions the PCI stood aside from the popular anti-fascist resistance. On the 29th of October 1922 the Italian King Victor Emmanuel III invited Mussolini to form a government. The next day Mussolini arrived in Rome following a small, poorly coordinated group of fascist demonstrators most of whom arrived by train, which the vainglorious Mussolini dubbed the 'march on Rome'.

From *The Times* and the *Daily Mail* to the Prime Minister, Bonar Law, the British establishment greeted Mussolini's rise to power with unconcealed delight. As early as December 1922 Mussolini was in London dining with King George V at Buckingham Palace. In 1923 George V further endorsed the regime by becoming one of the first heads of state to visit Mussolini's Rome. One of the most admiring tributes came from Sylvia's old foe Winston Churchill. In 1927, after widespread fascist violence, including the murder of high-profile opponents, and the establishment of a dictatorship, Churchill told Mussolini at a press conference in Rome, 'Your movement has rendered a service to the whole world', that Italy provided an example 'to defend the honour and stability of civilised society', continuing, 'If I had been an Italian I should have been wholeheartedly with you from start to finish in your triumphant struggle against the bestial appetites and passions of Leninism.'[3]

The *Dreadnought* noted with alarm that immediately after the 'march on Rome', Italian fascists in London marched to Westminster Abbey dressed in the fascist black shirts to lay a wreath on the tomb of the unknown warrior.[4] Not all Italians in London supported the fascists, and Silvio was involved with immigrant Italian anti-fascists, as well as London's only Italian anti-fascist publication, *Il Comento*, which ran from 1922 to 1924.[5] Silvio and Sylvia frequented 'King Bomba', the grocer's shop in Soho run by the Italian anarchist Emidio Recchioni, which doubled up as a radical meeting space.[6] However, the organised Italian anti-fascists remained in a minority. *La Cronaca*, the Italian weekly published in London, became openly fascist and the fascists were able to boast prominent restaurant owners among their members and a headquarters in Soho. Not everyone who joined was pro-fascist, some joined because they felt it would help their businesses, others were attracted by the idea of national unity, and some were intimidated into it.[7]

Even amongst British liberals and left reformists there was ambiguity about the nature of fascism, as Sylvia's son would remember: 'many people continued to see it as an absurdity of the Italians. They didn't see it as a real threat.'[8] The famous liberal historian George Macaulay Trevelyan took precisely this approach arguing in 1923 that Italians were not culturally predisposed to elections.[9] Meanwhile, the Labour Party leadership held that the Italian workers' militancy had been partly to blame for the rise of fascism.[10]

Sylvia, who had witnessed early fascist violence in Bologna in 1919, had kept abreast of Italian political developments through communist activity and through Corio's contacts. She was one of the first people in Britain to analyse emerging Italian fascism, warn of the threat it posed beyond Italy, and to organise anti-fascist campaigns. One of the striking things about Sylvia's analysis was her insistence from as early as November 1922 that fascism was a creation of capitalism: 'The White Terror has been experienced to the full in Finland and Hungary, but that was the White Terror of the old aristocracy. Fascism is the White Terror of modern Capitalism.'[11]

Fascism was the form of modern counter-revolution; the best weapon for a ruling class terrified of Bolshevism. Therefore, from the outset Sylvia understood that fascism was not 'an absurdity of the Italians', instead it posed a dangerous threat across Europe. In April 1923 the *Dreadnought*'s introduction to its front page article 'The Hooked Cross in Austria', written by the Austrian Jewish novelist Andreas Latzko, explained that the swastika 'is the emblem of the German Fascisti, standing for aggressive nationalism, anti-Semitism, and anti-Socialism'.[12] Sylvia was thus at the forefront of drawing attention to fascism in both Italy and Germany.

At first she challenged those on the left who held illusions about Mussolini's project. Immediately after Mussolini's 'march on Rome' Hamilton Fyfe, editor of the *Daily Herald*, wrote 'It is impossible not to feel a certain amount of admiration for this man who has organised what he calls a bloodless revolution.'[13] Sylvia cited the fascist record of murders, beatings, destruction and vicious humiliation of opponents. A PCI secretary 'was seized by Fascisti, who shaved his head and beard, painted the Italian national colours on his head, and dragged him through the streets'.[14] She wrote of a favourite fascist tactic of dragging opponents, male and female, into the streets and forcing them to drink castor oil causing immediate and extreme diarrhoea.[15] She also identified that the political repression would go far beyond repressing the far left. In 1928 and 1935 she engaged in lengthy correspondence with George Bernard Shaw who declared himself more in favour of Mussolini's 'Corporate State' than 'Liberal bourgeois democracy'. Sylvia pointed out that in Italy 'Industry remains in the hands of the Capitalists as it always did', adding that if Shaw lived in Italy he too would probably have been a victim of fascism.[16] From the outset Sylvia insisted that Mussolini would establish a dictatorship and that any opposition was perceived as a legitimate target by the fascists. She noted that in the 'march on Rome', fascists 'invaded the newspaper offices, destroyed the machinery, even of Capitalist papers opposed to them, and terrorised the editors with firearms'.[17]

It was her appreciation of the threat of fascism that forced Sylvia to break with aspects of her abstentionist politics, while her former ally Bordiga, though resolutely anti-fascist, continued to entertain the idea that social democracy was the bigger threat to the working class even in the months before Mussolini took power, writing 'So the fascists want to burn down the parliamentary circus? We'd love to see the day! ... The main danger is, and remains, that everyone agrees that the apple cart isn't overturned, and that a legal and parliamentary solution is found.'[18]

Sylvia, however, saw fascism as the most fundamental threat to the European working class and therefore approached figures from across liberal and labour circles to participate in the anti-fascist campaigns she initiated. In the early 1920s she and Silvio were instrumental in founding the organisation Friends of Italian Freedom League. Also involved were Labour MPs George Lansbury, James Maxton, C.P. Trevelyan and Josiah Wedgwood, the pacifists Fenner Brockway and Bertrand Russell, and the writers H.G. Wells and Rebecca West, while Silvio brought in the Italian anti-fascists around 'King Bomba' and the *Il Comento* publication.[19]

In 1924 the violence of Mussolini's regime was brought back into the spotlight when the socialist deputy Giacomo Matteotti was kidnapped and murdered by fascists. Eleven days earlier he had made a speech in the Chamber amidst heckling and

Sylvia addressing an anti-fascist demonstration in Hyde Park. (© Bundesarchiv, Bild Y 1-402/90)

intimidation denouncing fascist violence and corruption. He left the Chamber telling a colleague 'you can prepare for my funeral oration'.[20] One year after his murder the Friends of Italian Freedom League organised a commemoration for Matteotti which they held, confidently and courageously, in St James' Hall on Greek Street in Soho, the same district as the fascists' headquarters.[21]

FROM LEFTWING COMMUNISM TO THIRD WORLDISM

In 1919 the First World War's victorious powers constructed the League of Nations, boasting of their commitment to peace, international cooperation and national self-determination. They simultaneously planned military intervention in Russia and demanded devastating reparations payments from Germany. Britain and France divided up former German colonies between themselves, snatching and redrawing large parts of the Middle East. However, they soon found themselves facing rebellions across their Empires.

How revolutionaries living in imperialist countries should relate to these uprisings was explored afresh at the 1920 Third International Congress, which Sylvia attended. Lenin introduced the topic which was described as 'one of the most important life-and-death questions for the Communist International'.[22] Tom Quelch, from the British delegation, complained that British workers would be hostile to calls to support uprisings against the British Empire. Against this the Bolsheviks argued that active solidarity with anti-imperialist movements was integral to fighting the imperialist powers at home: 'It is impossible for the British proletariat to free itself from the yoke imposed on it by capitalism unless it steps into the breach for the revolutionary colonial movement.'[23]

Drawing on Trotsky's theory of permanent revolution, the Bolsheviks also argued that because they were living in the age of capitalism it was not necessary for every country to individually endure a period of capitalist development before revolutionary socialist movements could emerge. After all, capitalism had not developed in the same way in every country: countries that newly industrialised did not start with the innovations of the 1800s; instead global trade enabled them to 'skip' intermediate stages of development to acquire the most advanced and modern innovations. Anticipating an age of revolution, the Bolsheviks argued that the working class in more economically developed countries could support revolutionary movements of workers and peasants in less economically developed countries to enable them to construct socialism without having first to subjugate their demands to a bourgeois revolution: 'Thus the masses of the backward countries may reach communism not through capitalist development but led by the class-conscious proletariat of the advanced countries.'[24]

Sylvia's commitment to equality and internationalism meant that her approach to anti-imperialism was much closer to the Bolshevik perspective than many of those on the British left such as Quelch. However, her belief that the growth of reformism only hampered the development of revolutionary consciousness led her increasingly to reject the idea of an alliance in which workers in developed countries could support other countries which, if left in isolation, would be unable to materially support a revolutionary, egalitarian state for their population. Instead, in a perspective that foreshadowed the development of 'Third Worldist' politics in the 1960s, she thought that underdeveloped countries where there was no social democracy would be more revolutionary than the working class in Western Europe. In the same way that she could only see reformism having a negative impact on revolutionary consciousness, she believed that oppression and tyranny positively aided the conditions for revolution, even arguing that conditions in Tsarist Russia were more conducive to revolution than in Britain:

> The Russians, who before the revolution, yet lived in a perpetual atmosphere of revolution, who, under the pressure of constant persecution, habitually employed conspirative methods and always hoped for insurrection, have difficulty perhaps in realising how much we, here in Britain, have to learn in these directions, how difficult it is

for our people to adjust their minds to real belief in revolution and to genuine preparation for it.[25]

These ideas were reflected in a book Sylvia wrote about India, published in Bombay in 1926.[26] Written at a time of huge protest movements, from non-cooperation to industrial unrest, to which the British government responded with massacres and intense political persecution, Sylvia's book was a savage indictment of British imperialism which totally undermined the argument that imperialism brought civilisation and advancement. However, she suggested no ways in which British workers could support the Indian workers and it is instructive that the book was only published in India.

While Sylvia did continue to campaign in Britain, she focused less and less on organising in the working class. Her changing orientation was reflected in several decisions she made in the 1920s. She moved out of working-class Bow to the East London suburb of Woodford, in Essex, where she and Corio attempted to run a tea-shop in the home they christened the 'Red Cottage'. In 1924 she finally wound up the *Dreadnought* and for a short time ran a cultural journal titled *Germinal*. Sylvia was not directly involved in the 1926 general strike, although she did take practical steps of support by looking after the children of striking Welsh miners at the Red Cottage and finding other strikers' children temporary homes in East London.[27]

THE FAMILY: THE PERSONAL IS POLITICAL

The struggle for political equality had encouraged women to imagine radical changes in other aspects of their lives. In the suffragette movement there were a number of lesbians and women who remained unmarried and constructed their own alternative kinds of families.[28] The difficulties created in Sylvia's relationship with Keir Hardie because Hardie was married almost certainly fuelled Sylvia's own objections to the institution of marriage.

After the Russian Revolution Sylvia began to publicly explore radical ideas about personal relationships. She studied the profound changes to women's lives in Russia and was in contact and political sympathy with Alexandra Kollontai who, as head of the Women's Department of the Bolshevik Party in the early 1920s, encouraged and implemented these changes. In the 1920s Sylvia advocated the kind of relationships that were being formed in the new Russia:

> We believe that marriage should not be the subject of legal contract.
> We are for free sexual unions, contracted and terminated at will.
> We believe that no obstacle to the union of love should be admitted.
> We believe that loveless unions should not be maintained.[29]

She predicted that in the future humans would generally choose monogamy, but she adopted an open-minded approach, arguing that people ought to be free to determine their own lives subject only to mutual consent:

> Sexual love, like any other sort of love, will be a private matter, left to the decision of those, and only those, immediately concerned. Should there be cases in which a man loves more than one woman, or a woman more than one man, the affair will be solved according to the desires of the lovers and of the loved. Should they find themselves able to share their mutual affection, no social opprobrium or interference will result.[30]

Defying the social pressure, Sylvia did not marry Silvio Corio, with whom she lived until his death in 1954. In 1927, at the age of 45, Sylvia was pregnant with the child she so dearly wanted. Born in December 1927, Richard Keir Pethick Pankhurst was named after the people who had inspired and been closest to Sylvia: her father, Keir Hardie and Emmeline Pethick-Lawrence.

At the same time that Sylvia was developing a political understanding of personal relationships so, in a very different way, was Emmeline Pankhurst. Echoing the approach of Christabel outlined in *The Great Scourge*, which urged a change in individual behaviour as opposed to social change, Emmeline spent the 1920s lecturing in Canada for the Canadian

National Council for Combating Venereal Disease. She blamed
sexual diseases on promiscuity which she linked with the rise
of Bolshevism.[31] Emmeline refused to see Sylvia when she
came to visit, and was terrified of the effect the controversy of
Sylvia's position as an unmarried mother might have on her new
campaign.[32] Emmeline was at that time standing for election
to Parliament as the Conservative Party candidate, but died
in June 1928, nearly a year before the general election. Some
of Emmeline's supporters, both then and now, went as far as
to at least partially blame Sylvia for her death.[33] Sylvia was
marginalised from commemorations of her mother's life, and
despite being the only one of Emmeline's daughters to be in
England when a statue of Emmeline was unveiled in 1930, she
was pointedly excluded from the list of speakers, which included
the former Conservative Prime Minister.

Richard's birth prompted Sylvia to develop her thinking about
maternity, as she would recall:

> My little son nestled his rosy face against my breast.
> The doctor stood beside me:
> 'If you had not come into the [nursing] home when you did, baby could
>   not have been born.'
> The words came to me as a challenge:
> 'Seek to obtain for others the care you had!'[34]

Three years later she published a campaigning book titled *Save
the Mothers: A Plea for Measures to Prevent the Annual Loss
of about 3000 Child-bearing Mothers and 20,000 Infant Lives
in England and Wales and a Similar Grievous Wastage in other
Countries*. It was a pioneering political analysis of maternity
that exploded the myth that the way mothers were treated was
inevitable, arguing that it instead reflected contemporary political
and social attitudes to women. Mother and infant mortality
rates were highest in society's most oppressed groups: poor and
unemployed mothers. The book broke radical new ground,
particularly over the question of abortion. Responding to a
medical authority calling for it to be compulsory to register all
abortions, Sylvia wrote that this could only be accomplished by a

change in the law: 'obviously whilst abortion remains a criminal offence it will always be concealed if deliberately induced, and there will be a certain amount of hesitation in disclosing it, even if it has happened spontaneously'.[35] Sylvia considered abortion from the perspective of the women concerned and drew on her wide experience of working with poor women in the East End:

> Numerous indeed are the married women in this country who, under economic pressure and the strain of maintaining the welfare of their families, have attempted abortion, not once but many times. 'When I found I was pregnant again I tried everything!' How often that phrase slips out when a mother is telling her troubles to sympathetic ears![36]

While stating that the only real solution was fundamental social change, she drew upon her knowledge of Russia to consider two reforms that could immediately improve women's lives:

> Mothers vehemently defend abortion, declaring that they have resorted to it for the sake of their children. Increasing numbers of people argue that, faced with undesired pregnancy, women will procure abortion by hook or by crook; therefore the law should permit abortion, provided it be done under State supervision, with strict aseptic precautions. Others consider that since even under the best conditions abortion is injurious to the mother, it should be avoided by preventing pregnancy, and that the use of contraceptives should be publicly taught under Government auspices. Both views have received legislative sanction in Soviet Russia, which in this, as in much else, has become a field of experiment in social theories.[37]

Sixteen years before the establishment of the National Health Service, Sylvia called for 'an entirely free and efficient maternity service open to all',[38] and in many ways she envisaged a far more progressive system than women experience today. She called for maternity benefits equivalent to the mother's wage for five months before the birth and a year after (and 'similar payments in case of an abortion or still-birth until the patient is restored to health'); safeguards that no woman be dismissed by their employer for failure to work during pregnancy or for a year after birth; mothers' benefits to enable them to look after their children up to the age of at least five if they so wanted, and cooperative housekeeping and nurseries to enable mothers who wanted to continue their professions to do so.[39]

The book, which won a supportive review from the feminist writer Vera Brittain, demonstrated Sylvia's continuing commitment to women's rights.

RECLAIMING THE SUFFRAGETTES:
SYLVIA AND WOMEN'S FIGHT AGAINST FASCISM

Sylvia's understanding of fascism as a totally reactionary force enabled her to see that it would violently deprive women of their rights. Women's 'newfound emancipation', she wrote, 'has gone down in the shipwreck of Democracy. Fascism and Dictatorship, resting not on the consent of the people, but on military power, are intrinsically the enemies of the women's movement.'[40] A petition she launched in 1932 protested at Mussolini forcing out all women professors in Italy, and after Hitler took power she wrote a chapter on 'Women under the Nazis' in her series 'Fascism as it is'. She examined the degrading torture of women opponents of the Nazis, the forced sterilisation schemes, the throwing out of women from the professions, and warned that in Hitler's Germany women were viewed as 'mere breeding machines'.[41]

She also saw a special role for women in anti-fascism. In 1932 she established the Women's International Matteotti Committee (WIMC) to campaign against the fascist persecution of Velia Matteotti, Giacomo Matteotti's widow. The Matteotti home was kept under constant police surveillance; the children were forbidden to use their father's name in school, where Matteotti's eldest son was forced to sing fascist hymns and salute Mussolini's portrait. The children were also forbidden from visiting his grave (which was frequently desecrated), and anyone who dared to visit them had their details taken and was at risk of imprisonment.[42]

Although she no longer looked to build a mass campaign, Sylvia was able to attract significant figures to lend public support. In particular, the WIMC relied strongly upon the support of veterans from the women's suffrage campaign; as well as Sylvia one of the founders was ex-ELFS member Charlotte Drake, and members included the Irish former suffragette Hannah Sheehy Skeffington, as well as American women's suffrage activists Alice Stone Blackwell, Harriot Stanton Blatch and Rose Schneiderman, the labour organiser and women's suffrage supporter Sylvia met on her American suffrage tour. Towards the end of 1932 the WIMC organised an international petition calling for Velia Matteotti's freedom with signatories from across the left, feminist and pacifist movements. It included a significant number of former leading suffragettes (Emmeline Pethick-Lawrence, Charlotte Despard, Dora Montefiore and Evelyn Sharp) and some of the suffragettes' most prominent male supporters (George Lansbury, Laurence Housman and Henry Nevinson). Sylvia was also centrally involved in establishing the Women's Committee against War and Fascism, of which she was the treasurer, while former suffragette Hannah Laurie was its secretary.[43] When later campaigning for the independence of Italy's former colonies she got the suffragette's first window smasher, Mary Leigh, to take part.[44]

Involving these former suffragettes can partly be attributed to Sylvia drawing on personal contacts. However, mobilising veteran suffragettes was also directly connected to Sylvia's understanding of the suffragette struggle, which in the 1930s was back on her mind – in this decade she wrote her renowned work *The Suffragette Movement: An Intimate Account of Persons and Ideals* (1931), and an assessment of her mother's role, *The Life of Emmeline Pankhurst: The Suffragette Struggle for Women's Citizenship* (1936). In 1918 the four years of war and the prioritisation of nationalism by significant sections of the women's movement had enabled the government to present the granting of women's suffrage as a celebration of women's wartime patriotism and remove it from the prewar militant suffragette movement, particularly its working-class, socialist sections such as the one led by Sylvia. The suffragettes never got to claim their victory, there was no triumphant demonstration, nor a day of reckoning for the politicians who had forced them to endure so much horror. When the vote was granted on equal terms with men in

1928 the suffragettes again went unacknowledged, the extension of the franchise being popularly described and patronised as the 'flapper vote'. Sylvia has been criticised for prudish criticism of women in the 1920s and 1930s, for being unable to relate to a generation of women who embraced increased leisure time, make up and short skirts, chastising them for being politically disengaged, individualistically concerned with their own careers and earning more money.[45] But Sylvia was not criticising personal behaviour, and she herself took advantage of the more free and practical shorter skirts and hair (she did however disapprove of make up); rather, she was attacking attempts to reduce the struggle for women's liberation to an apolitical, commercialised individualism. In fact, the struggle had been motivated by a desire for profound social change and democracy. Now that democracy and all the gains that women had made were threatened by the rise of fascism, it was the anti-fascist struggle that represented the real tradition of the militant suffrage movement. In 1936 she wrote in the *Daily Herald*: 'Daily I receive letters from women ... [who] appeal to me to know what they can do and urge me to give a lead which will enable them to come together to struggle for international justice as women struggled for national justice in their fight for the vote.'[46]

Sylvia did give a lead engaging women in the struggle against fascist militarism. This resulted in a very positive assessment of contemporary women's political engagement. On the eve of the 1935 general election, when women were the majority of the electorate, Sylvia wrote:

> The women's own outlook has largely changed. Before we were voters, it was only the few who took any real interest in politics, the majority felt that the issues of the election were outside their province. To-day the average woman is as keen as her husband and brother on the great political issues by which the Governments stand or fall. On many questions she is better informed than the average man.
>
> Peace is the issue which grips every woman voter.[47]

Sylvia's mobilisation of women in opposition to fascism helped reclaim the radical, democratic suffragette tradition.

7

Fighting Imperialism in War and Peace

Sylvia started the 1930s campaigning for peace. In 1930 she joined the Women's International League for Peace and Freedom, and the International Peace Crusade. She was also the treasurer of the Women's World International Committee Against War and Fascism.[1] By the end of the decade she concluded that a war was needed to defeat fascism. Although this might appear superficially to resemble the trajectory of her longstanding opponents such as Winston Churchill, her changing campaigning priorities reflected her consistent opposition to fascism and an understanding of 'war' and 'peace' that was completely at odds with the British government's. The radical interpretations of imperialism, war and resistance with which Sylvia identified would come to shape the postwar world and Sylvia's last great campaign.

APPEASEMENT MEANS WAR

In the 1880s Italy joined the 'Scramble for Africa' and snatched territory in East Africa which became Italian Somaliland and Eritrea. These colonies bordered the ancient kingdom of Ethiopia, but the Italian attempt to colonise Ethiopia was abandoned after the Ethiopians inflicted a devastating defeat on the Italian army at the battle of Adwa in March 1896. Ethiopia therefore remained the only African state to have maintained its independence from nineteenth-century European colonialism.[2]

In the 1920s and 1930s Ethiopia was a rapidly modernising nation, encouraged by the Regent Ras Tafari who in 1930 was crowned Ethiopian Emperor Haile Selassie I. There were huge strides made in education for boys and girls, a printing press was established, a written constitution was introduced and legislation passed to phase out slavery. In September 1923 Ethiopia was admitted to the League of Nations as a member state. This seemed to guarantee Ethiopia's independent future as the League's stated purpose was to protect its member states' sovereignty and replace war with arbitration.

For Mussolini, who fantasised about building a new Roman Empire, Ethiopia, situated next to two other Italian colonies, was a perfect target. The first shots were fired on the 5th of December 1934 at Wal Wal – an oasis far inside Ethiopian territory in the Ogaden desert which Italy had seized with Somalian troops. When the Ethiopians withdrew, after over a hundred of their troops had been killed, Italy demanded the Ethiopians apologise, pay them damages, punish the Ethiopian troops involved and that an Ethiopian delegation salute the Italian flag at Wal Wal – which would amount to a recognition of Italian sovereignty over the territory.[3] The Ethiopians refused and requested the League of Nations arbitrate between the two member states; but the Ethiopians soon discovered that some member states were more equal than others. In January 1935 the French Foreign Minister Pierre Laval met with Mussolini and privately indicated there would be no French opposition to an Italian invasion of Ethiopia.[4] The British government's true feelings were expressed in the secret report it commissioned Sir John Maffey to write in June 1935, which cynically concluded that there were 'no vital British interests in Abyssinia* or adjacent countries such as to necessitate British resistance to an Italian conquest of Abyssinia'.[5] A month later the British government placed an arms embargo on East Africa, ostensibly to defuse the situation. But in practice this massively favoured the well-armed fascists and stopped weapons from going to poorly armed Ethiopia which was appealing for help in its self-defence.

On the 3rd of October 1935, confident of the complicity of Britain and France, Italy invaded Ethiopia. The League of

---

* In Europe at this time Ethiopia was commonly referred to as 'Abyssinia', despite the fact that the people who lived there called it Ethiopia. Sylvia referred to the country as Ethiopia.

Nations imposed some sanctions on Italy but crucially they did not extend to coal, iron, steel or oil – all vitally important materials for conducting modern warfare.[6] Indeed, Mussolini later told Hitler that had an oil sanction been imposed he would have been forced to withdraw his forces from Ethiopia within a week.[7] The other decisive measure would have been to close the British-controlled Suez Canal, thereby blocking all supplies to the fascist army, but the British government refused, pledging the sanctity of business – which happened to be making a tidy profit from the new Italian traffic.[8]

The British and French governments thought that appeasing Mussolini's ambitions in Ethiopia – which would not adversely affect their 'interests' – would prevent Mussolini being driven into an alliance with Hitler, whose ambitions for German expansion in Europe would threaten British and French power.

Sylvia argued that this was a completely counter-productive approach. From the end of 1934 she bombarded the press with letters arguing that appeasing fascist governments would only strengthen, not lessen, the fascist threat: 'Let these doubting ones not suppose that to allow the Italian Fascist Government to do its bloody worst in Africa would save Europe from war. The success of Fascist arms there would be but the prelude to other adventures and greater daring.'[9]

She dismissed the argument that opposing Mussolini would result in Italy declaring war on Britain, pointing out that had sanctions affecting military capability been imposed on Italy it would not have been able to invade Ethiopia, let alone contemplate attacking elsewhere.[10] She argued that far from distancing Mussolini from Hitler, allowing him to invade Ethiopia would strengthen the expansionist ambitions of both powers who would unite around their common, anti-democratic ideology, asking foresightedly 'is the whole affair to be hushed up to fester until the crime of assenting to this Fascist conquest bears fruit in a European war precipitated by the twin dictatorships of Italy and Germany?'[11] Appeasing fascism, therefore, would lead to war not peace, and resisting fascism would lead to peace not war.

MODERN TIMES

Sylvia responded to the Italian invasion of Ethiopia by launching a new newspaper in May 1936. She called it the *New Times and Ethiopia News* (*NTEN*), a title partly inspired by the film *Modern Times* by the anti-fascist actor Charlie Chaplin, which had been released earlier that year.[12] As in the *Dreadnought*, her paper gave space to new, radical voices; contributors included the anti-racist author Nancy Cunard, Dr Harold Moody of the League of Coloured People, Ethiopian writers, Italian anti-fascists, and leading figures in the Pan African movement. One account of her paper described it as conveying 'by far the most copious and widely distributed information about affairs in Ethiopia of any news source in the world'.[13] She printed exclusive reports on the Ethiopian resistance that challenged the indifference of the mainstream media. A West African student in Britain wrote to tell her that 'if it were not for your paper the young Africans would not know what is happening in Africa today, as the whole of the press in Europe has no room to publish the Ethiopian case', a sentiment that Sylvia's son described as 'typical of the African response'.[14] Despite the censorship, and the fascists' suspension of telegraph services, her paper carried reports of the three-day massacre in Addis Ababa in which thousands of Ethiopians were killed in revenge for an attempt on the life of the fascist commander Graziani.[15] During the invasion of Ethiopia the *NTEN* played an important role in undermining the fascist propaganda that Italy was on a 'civilising mission'. Sylvia exposed the war crimes committed by the fascists, especially the bombing of red cross units and the use of poison gas by the Italian Air Force.[16]

In 1936 Sylvia also campaigned against aerial bombardment by commissioning a unique monument. The 'stone bomb' by sculptor Eric Benfield was unveiled in Woodford, sarcastically dedicated 'to those who in 1932 upheld the right to use bombing planes in outlying districts', which referred to the failure of the Disarmament Conference to ban aerial bombing. Since the 1920s in Iraq, Britain had used bombing raids to crush rebellions.

Sylvia saw aerial warfare as 'cruelly unfair methods of gassing and bombing the innocent', perceiving the tendency of twentieth-century warfare to target civilians.[17] The stone bomb was unveiled a year before Guernica, several years before the London Blitz and the Allied bombing of German cities in the Second World War, and nearly ten years before American forces dropped the atom bombs on Japan – something that Sylvia would later say 'adds an appalling new terror to war', particularly because it would be Japan's people that would 'suffer for the sin of their rulers'.[18] Once again, Sylvia was able to identify the trajectory of warfare in 'modern times', because it happened first in Ethiopia.

FIGHTING FASCISM: SPAIN AND THE EAST END

As Sylvia predicted, the tragedy that unfolded in Ethiopia was now re-enacted in Europe. In July 1936 General Franco led a fascistic revolt from within the Spanish army against the republican government of Spain. Once again the British and French governments claimed 'neutrality', refusing to sell weapons to either side. This indirectly benefited Franco's superior military forces which were being given massive support from Mussolini and Hitler. The British and French governments stood aside, making no effort to defend the elected Spanish government. Sylvia linked the betrayal of Spain with that of Ethiopia, attributing both to the prejudices of rightwingers who felt more threatened by black people and republicanism than by fascism:

> People stood by while Ethiopia was vanquished: this is only Africa: this is not a White Man's country. They listened to the Italian propaganda: these are primitives, their customs are barbarous. Now people stand by again: they do not like Spanish politics; these are a disorderly people, fighting amongst themselves; they are Anarchists, Socialists, Reds, strikers; it does not matter to us.[19]

The complacency of the British government was demonstrated as late as January 1939, three months before Franco declared victory in Spain, when Sylvia participated in a women's delegation organised by the All London Aid Spain Council to the Foreign Office and were told that the government's priority was to prevent the civil war becoming an international war. Sylvia responded 'It is an international war!'[20] Indeed it was an international war as thousands of anti-fascists from 53 countries defied their passive or pro-fascist governments to travel to Spain and fight in the International Brigades against Franco.[21]

In Britain the East End of London quickly became a centre of anti-fascist activity. The Communist Party, which was the backbone of the International Brigades, was developing a popular base in East London. As Phil Piratin, who would be elected as Communist Party MP for East London in 1945, recalled: 'Stepney is proud to record that the first three Britons to fight with the Spanish people against the fascists were Stepney boys.'[22] At the same time the large Jewish community in East London was increasingly coming under attack from Oswald Mosley's British Union of Fascists (BUF). On the 4th of October 1936 the Communist Party, Jewish organisations and trade unions mobilised hundreds of thousands of local people to stop the BUF from marching through the parts of the East End where the Jewish community lived. Despite the violence of the mounted police who were trying to clear a way for the BUF march, the anti-fascist demonstration, which took inspiration from the Spanish anti-fascist slogan '*No Pasaran*' ('they shall not pass'), was victorious. The day became known as the legendary 'Battle of Cable Street'.

The *NTEN* reported extensively on developments in Spain and also carried reports of the East End resistance to fascism. However, beyond this, despite the growing movement of working-class anti-fascism emerging in the very part of London that Sylvia knew so well, she did not seek to get deeply involved. There were probably several reasons for this. First and foremost her decision to focus on Ethiopia reflected her concern that Ethiopia would be overlooked in the anti-fascist struggle. Indeed prominent anti-fascist figures even argued that it should be, the famous journalist H.N. Brailsford writing: 'Spain interests us more than Ethiopia. Of course, the Ethiopians, victims of an unjust aggression, have claim on our sympathy and assistance. Yet, after all, their feudal monarchy has nothing to offer civilisation.'[23] Sylvia published a reply by an Ethiopian student on the front page of the NTEN which stated 'we shall not be unjust to Spain, by being just to Ethiopia' and reminded readers that in the nineteenth century Marx and Engels espoused the cause of backward nations fighting Russian imperialism.[24]

Justifying the importance of the Ethiopian cause also required confronting racism and imperialism by insisting that occupation and oppression must be opposed whomsoever is subjected to it. But only part of the increased willingness to champion Spain could be put down to racist or colonialist assumptions – Spain was also able to galvanise support in Britain more easily because of greater political sympathy with its republican government, because it was far easier to get to than Ethiopia, and because there was far greater internal radicalism in Spain which therefore resonated more naturally with the British left. However, beyond reporting on Spain, Sylvia did not make significant attempts to integrate her pro-Ethiopian propaganda within British working-class anti-fascism. Upon starting the NTEN she made it clear she did not see it as something which would relate to a mass, working-class audience. Instead, as she told a colleague, the proposed newspaper 'could be sent to Members of Parliament, Members of the Government, Editors of newspapers, and other persons of influence'.[25]

This decision was probably due in part to the increasingly pessimistic assessment she came to in the 1920s of the Western European working-class as an agent for self-emancipation. However, it can also probably be attributed to the fact that the Communist Party was so dominant in the Spanish and East End agitation at a time when Sylvia saw the leadership from Russia as more than just counter-productive, as she had done in the early 1920s – now, under Stalin, it had become counter-revolutionary. This probably explains why in all her anti-fascist campaigning she was able to work with many she had disagreed with in the Labour Party, but seemed to steer clear of anyone in the Communist Party.

SYLVIA TAKES ON STALIN

One of the things generally overlooked about the *NTEN* is the fact that it consistently articulated a far-left critique of Stalin. This also at a time when there was considerable pressure on anti-fascists to refrain from criticism as Stalin's Russia was the only external force arming the Spanish republicans. The *NTEN*, however, did not see Stalin as a principled opponent of fascism, something that was borne out in 1939 when Russian Foreign Minister Molotov and German Foreign Minister Ribbentrop secretly signed a non-aggression pact agreeing to divide Eastern Europe between them. In the *NTEN* Silvio Corio denounced the Pact thus: 'A clear and unmistakable declaration this, exposing once and for all the notion that even any residual particle of Socialism remains in Russia to-day under Stalin's rule.'[26]

In 1940 the *NTEN* ran a series of articles titled 'The Execution of the Old Bolsheviks', exposing the system of torture, blackmail and terror that lay behind Stalin's show trials of the former leadership of the Bolshevik Party.[27] Sylvia's son later recalled: 'During Stalin's time she spoke with horror of the purges, and particularly the trial of Bukharin and other old Bolsheviks, several of whom she had met in Moscow a decade or so earlier, and in whose alleged self-confessed treason she found it impossible to believe.'[28] When the exiled revolutionary Leon Trotsky was murdered in Mexico in 1940 on Stalin's orders, the *NTEN* reported it on the front page. The article was written by Peter Petroff, the veteran of the 1905 revolution who had worked with Sylvia during the First World War before leaving for Russia after the revolution. By 1940 he was an exile in Britain again, this time from Stalin. At a time when Trotsky had been totally demonised by Stalin's government, the front page of the *NTEN* told of the intense persecution of Trotsky's entire family and declared: 'So Stalin's axe has struck at the head of the indefatigable revolutionary! A brain that could not be subdued nor corrupted had to be knocked out.'[29]

ANTI-IMPERIALISM AND THE EMPEROR

Before Italy entered the Second World War the main focus of Sylvia's campaigning was to try to force the British government to oppose Italy's invasion of Ethiopia and to see Ethiopia recognised as a victim of fascist aggression.

The Ethiopian Emperor Haile Selassie left Addis Ababa on 2 May 1936 as the fascist army approached, but although he was evacuated by a British warship this stopped at Gibraltar on the false pretence that the warship was in need of repair. The Emperor, transported to Britain on a passenger liner, was therefore prevented from arriving as an important or official guest.[30] This was demanded by the Italian ambassador whom the British government readily appeased, denying Haile Selassie an official welcome when he arrived by train at Waterloo station. Nevertheless there was a welcome party, which included Sylvia who presented Haile Selassie with a copy of her newspaper and a Memorial of Welcome signed by the *NTEN* journalists.[31] Haile Selassie spent most of his time in Britain far away from London in Bath, largely ignored by the British government who found his presence embarrassing. However, Sylvia continued to visit him and print his pronouncements in her paper; the *NTEN* was the only newspaper to print his 1936 address to the League of Nations Assembly in full.[32]

Some historians have struggled to understand how Sylvia, a republican, could have worked so willingly with the Emperor of Ethiopia, some even postulating that Haile Selassie was a 'father figure' to her.[33] Apart from being extremely patronising, this totally ignores the context in which she worked with the Emperor. In fact she made the terms perfectly clear on one of her first meetings with Haile Selassie, as her son recalled: 'my mother explained that she was a republican, and did not support him because he was an Emperor, but because "his cause was just." He quietly replied, "I know!"'[34] Moreover, Sylvia insisted that the Emperor should be treated as a sympathetic head of state by the British government, not because she like pomp and ceremony, but because she realised that the British government's refusal to do so was integral to their continuing appeasement of Mussolini. Her fears were well-grounded. On the 2nd of November 1938 the British government recognised the Italian 'conquest' of Ethiopia, and accepted the Italian King Victor Emmanuel as the 'Emperor of Ethiopia', despite the fact that the Ethiopians never surrendered and continued to resist throughout the Italian occupation. Sylvia's newspaper therefore emphasised that Haile Selassie was the Ethiopian Emperor and reported on the Ethiopian resistance.

However, the desire to appease Mussolini was only one part of the British establishment's indifference to Ethiopia; as one politician bluntly expressed it in his diary: 'I am bored by this Italian-Abyssinian dispute, and I really fail to see why we should interfere ... Why should England fight over Abyssinia, when most of our far flung Empire has been won by conquest.'[35] To the British government, the Italian invasion looked like simple colonialism, to which they had no objection so long as it did not threaten British interests. By taking up the cause of Ethiopia, therefore, Sylvia had to go beyond anti-fascism and challenge colonialism. Indeed, while relatively few anti-fascists remained concerned with Ethiopia, the Ethiopian cause was centrally important to black activists across the world. It was therefore this anti-colonialist movement, and not the British anti-fascist movement, that Sylvia would become most closely involved with in her campaign.

Ethiopia was a symbol for black anti-imperialists because it emerged as the only independent African country from nineteenth-century imperialism. For some, Haile Selassie's high-profile coronation in 1930 seemed the fulfilment of the Biblical prophecy 'Kings will come out of Africa'.[36] The way in which the invasion of Ethiopia galvanised anti-colonialist sentiments was conveyed by Kwame Nkrumah, who later became the first President of Ghana, when he described hearing the news whilst living in Britain:

on the [newspaper] placard I read: '*MUSSOLINI INVADES ETHIOPIA*'. That was all I needed. At that moment it was almost as if the whole of London had suddenly declared war on me personally. For the next few minutes I could do nothing but glare at each impassive face wondering if those people could possibly realise the wickedness of colonialism, and praying that the day might come when I could play my part in bringing about the downfall of such a system. My nationalism surged to the fore.[37]

From the start of the Italian invasion Sylvia was in touch with black activists championing the Ethiopian cause. In August 1935 Jomo Kenyatta, the future first President and Prime Minister of Kenya, wrote to inform her of the establishment of the International Friends of Abyssinia of which he was the honorary secretary, C.L.R. James was the chair, and Amy Ashwood Garvey, the widow of Marcus Garvey, was the treasurer.[38] Sylvia frequently worked and shared platforms with this organisation, and leading figures in the emerging Pan African movement, including Kenyatta, Wallace Johnston, T.R. Makonnen and George Padmore, read her paper and corresponded regularly with her.[39] Although Sylvia had started the *NTEN* to influence British politicians, it soon gained a popular readership with a wide circulation in the West Indies and West Africa, where its articles were reprinted in newspapers across the region. By May 1939 the British Colonial Secretary in Sierra Leone had the publication banned.[40] Championing the cause of Ethiopia, as the Colonial Secretary realised, inevitably provided inspiration to colonised people across the world.

ITALIAN ANTI-FASCISM AFTER ITALY DECLARED WAR

When Italy declared war on Britain on the 10th of June 1940 there was jubilation in Sylvia's home. Her son later wrote:

That Sunday, I recall, several Italian anti-Fascist refugees had come for dinner, as they often did at weekends, 'for a plate of macaroni', and we turned on the BBC evening news after it had begun. The announcer was reading out some uninteresting news after which he proceeded to give a 'fuller report of Signor Mussolini's declaration of war'. These words struck guests and hosts like an electric shock which gave way to a feeling of relief, and hope for the future.[41]

Silvio Corio abandoned his usual practice of writing under a pseudonym, writing a column exclaiming 'At last! The long, agonising vigil is over' and asserting 'the alignment is now complete'.[42] For Sylvia and Silvio, Mussolini's declaration of war raised the possibility of the complete assault on fascism they had campaigned so long for.

The day after Mussolini's declaration of war, the British Cabinet discussed what to do about the Italians in Britain who had now become 'enemy aliens'. Churchill ordered 'Collar the lot!'[43] But the British police did not 'collar the lot'; in fact, as Sylvia quickly exposed in the *NTEN*, ordinary Italians were rounded up while the wealthy, leading fascists were left alone. She reported that in one Soho café 'customers can hear the Italian proprietor expressing the hope that Hitler will take London'.[44] Headlines on the front page announced that the Italian fascist hymn was 'sung nightly at the "Roma" in Greek Street' and 'Founder of the Fascio in London Still at Large'.[45] After these revelations Sylvia was sent death threats. One signed 'Heil Hitler' threatened that unless the *NTEN* stopped publication it would 'find itself without an Editor'. Another signed 'Italian London Fascists' warned

Your house in Woodford will be bombed and burned to the ground. Hitler knows your address.
You will pay with your life if you publish any [fascist's] name in your paper.
Do not dare to go out in the dark or you will be murdered.
Heil Hitler.
Viva Mussolini.[46]

Her son recalls 'I think she didn't take it very seriously ... we didn't lock our back door at that time.'[47] Characteristically, she published the threats on the front page of the paper and continued with the exposés. Sylvia was later to find out that her name was in fact on the Gestapo list of those to arrest in the event of the Nazi invasion of Britain.

While the police were not arresting leading fascists, they were however interning leading anti-fascists. The *NTEN* protested as old acquaintances were rounded up, Silvio being saved perhaps because of his higher profile as a campaigner.[48] In fact, the Home Office and Security Services had been provided with a list of anti-fascists to *avoid* arresting, which Decio Anzani, the secretary of the Italian League for the Rights of Man and colleague of Silvio, had helped draw up.[49] The anti-fascists generally assumed that the arrests were not accidental on the part of a government who had long regarded the left as a greater threat than the fascists.[50] In July 1940 over a thousand interned prisoners were put on the *Arandora Star* ship to be deported to Canada. They included Italians, both fascist and anti-fascist, Germans and Austrians including Nazis and Jews. On July 2nd the boat was torpedoed by a German U-boat and over 700 lost their lives including Decio Anzani. The British government's report was a cover-up and no enquiry was ever held.[51]

LIBERATING ETHIOPIA FROM ITS 'LIBERATORS'

Mussolini's declaration of war changed Sylvia's campaigning priorities in a way that revealed the contradictions of the Second World War. The joy the anti-fascists had shared on hearing the news that Italy had joined the war reflected their desire to see an end to appeasement and to rid the world of fascism. Expressing this side of the struggle Sylvia wrote 'This is a people's war against dictatorship and must be fought as such by each and all who stand for liberty.' Evoking the spirit of internationalism that had been shown in the fight against Franco in Spain, Sylvia called for 'a new and greater international brigade'.[52] But the decisions in the war were taken by governments who had not abandoned their own private interests.[53]

Listening to the radio after Mussolini's declaration of war, Sylvia was shocked that Ethiopia's national anthem was not included in the 'National Anthems of Allies' weekly broadcast.

Sylvia therefore focused her energies on campaigning for Ethiopia to be recognised as an Ally by the British government. At first she was concerned that not gaining this status would result in the British government leaving Ethiopia as one of Italy's colonies. Indeed, even after the declaration of war the British government continued to recognise Victor Emmanuel as 'Emperor of Ethiopia'.[54] However, as the war drew on, her concern was that without Allied status Ethiopia would be colonised instead by the British. She was not the only person to have this on their mind; a Foreign Office memo relating to the demand to play the Ethiopian national anthem read 'Let us remember that what we are doing in Abyssinia is for our own benefit, not for that of the Abyssinians, and it is possible to imagine circumstances in which it might suit us to throw them over.'[55]

Agitating for the inclusion of the national anthem on the BBC was therefore part of an effort to safeguard Ethiopia's future. The issue also revealed the racist attitudes at the heart of the

Poster parade in 1946 outside the House of Commons exposing fascist war crimes in Ethiopia and demanding an end to colonial rule in the country. Sylvia is the second from the left.

British establishment. When Sylvia's parliamentary ally Geoffrey Mander, the MP for Wolverhampton East, raised a question in the House of Commons about the exclusion of the Ethiopian anthem, another MP retorted sarcastically 'Why could we not have the Wolverhampton National Anthem?'[56] A Foreign Office memo protested:

> The real absurdity of this proposal lies in the fact that not one person out of ten million, either here or in the Middle East, knows what the Abyssinian National Anthem is. However, neither this fact, nor the cruelty of inflicting discordant native music upon radio and other audiences, is likely to stop Mr Mander, Miss Pankhurst and others from pursuing this silly hare.[57]

Although Sylvia and Silvio generally looked for solutions 'from below' to the occupation of Ethiopia by calling for resistance in Italy and championing the resistance in Ethiopia, the long-term damage of appeasement which helped the fascist regimes grow more powerful convinced them, like many other anti-appeasement activists, that a full-scale war was necessary to defeat fascism. However, the interests of the resistance movements and of the Allied governments came into conflict when the Allied states adopted the role of 'liberator'. Although Sylvia was not opposed to the British government's intervention in Ethiopia she was sceptical about their intentions. After the Royal Air Force flew Haile Selassie back to Africa ahead of his return to Ethiopia, she regretted she had not had the chance to advise him 'not to trust our politicians at all and to get an agreement in writing, if possible, before leaving the country, as I feared that he was under the misapprehension that politicians are gentlemen in relation to political affairs which I have long learnt is seldom the case'.[58]

It was certainly not the case in Ethiopia, where the British government did not allow Haile Selassie and his Patriot forces to claim the liberation. Instead they 'liberated' Ethiopia with troops from racially segregated South Africa which Sylvia denounced as an ominous insult to the black Ethiopians fighting for freedom.[59] The Emperor was only able to arrive in the Ethiopian capital a month later in May 1941. Even then the country was kept under foreign occupation, the British informing Haile Selassie that he had no authority to appoint his own Cabinet.[60] Those who questioned this state of affairs were subjected to intimidation, as Haile Selassie's London secretary Ato Emmanuel Abraham discovered when he, alongside Sylvia, tried to alert British MPs to the British occupation of Ethiopia. He was summoned before Gilbert MacKereth, the colonel in charge of Ethiopian affairs who had been British Consul to Ethiopia during the Italian occupation. MacKereth 'assumed a serious attitude and said that I should not forget that it was wartime and that there was such a thing as detention'.[61] Three weeks after the *NTEN* reported on the 'Emperor's fight with his Liberators', the liberators cemented their intentions in the Anglo-Ethiopian Agreement of January 1942.[62] Although recognising Ethiopian independence, in practice it continued the British occupation, British forces remaining in control of the police, judiciary and communication networks, while British advisers were foisted on Haile Selassie's government.[63]

The problem Sylvia and other campaigners for Ethiopian freedom had in the 1940s was the same problem they faced in the 1930s: that the British establishment had no *ideological* opposition to fascism, especially if it was effectively repressing troublesome movements which, if unchecked, could spill out into wider anti-imperialist resistance. Sylvia's first visit to Ethiopia and Eritrea in 1944 allowed her to see first-hand that under the British occupation of Eritrea the Italian fascist police force was still in place, as were fascist laws; she saw notices in the cafés that still ordered 'Vietato per Nativi' (forbidden for natives).[64] Whilst there she became involved with the popular Eritrean movement to unite with Ethiopia, galvanised by the desire to escape fascist rule, and brutally repressed by the British occupation: after a pro-union demonstration shot at by the Italian police, 'the Chief British Administrator immediately issued a proclamation prohibiting the assembly of more than three persons, and forbidding the display of the Ethiopian flag or any badge concerned with Ethiopia'.[65]

Sylvia therefore agitated for the union of Ethiopia and Eritrea. She also campaigned for freedom from occupation across Africa. This gained her no popularity with the British government. An indication of official opinion can be seen in a letter from the Foreign Office official Daniel Lascelles, who in 1947 wrote to Harold Farquhar, the British minister in Addis Ababa: 'We agree wholeheartedly with you in your evident wish that this horrid old harridan should be choked to death with her own pamphlets.'[66]

More than thirty years after the end of the suffragette movement, Sylvia Pankhurst was still driving the British government to distraction.

REBUILDING ETHIOPIA

Sylvia's desire to build a better world forced her to spend most of her life fighting for the right of the working class, women, ethnic minorities, and people under imperialist occupations to be able to participate in determining the kind of world they lived in.

The Ethiopian struggle allowed her finally to become involved in constructing projects to improve peoples' lives. She initiated the Princess Tsehai Memorial Hospital Council to raise funds to establish Ethiopia's first modern teaching hospital, named in memory of Haile Selassie's daughter who had worked as a nurse in Britain, and was a friend of Sylvia's, but died in 1942.

She also helped Ethiopian students who came to Britain. In one remarkable instance a young student named Afewerk Tekle arrived in England with two other students and found no one to meet them. They were asked if they knew anyone in England and, as Sylvia's daughter-in-law later recounted, 'Well they didn't know anybody in England but Afewerk remembered that a woman had come to his school and that the teacher had shown [her] his sketchbooks and that her name was Pankhurst.'[67] Sylvia's son continued the story, relating, 'Well they telephoned and she said "send them round".'[68] Afewerk Tekle, 'almost as a son' to Sylvia, became one of Ethiopia's most famous artists.[69]

Silvio Corio died in 1954, and her old friend Emmeline Pethick-Lawrence in 1956, and so Sylvia made a new start by moving permanently with her son to Ethiopia in 1956. She edited a new paper, the *Ethiopia Observer*, and planned to improve the hospital she had been instrumental in founding.

When Sylvia died in 1960 she was buried in land allotted for Ethiopian Patriots in the grounds of Ethiopia's Holy Trinity Cathedral. She left behind a legacy of struggle in which she had always championed the cause of the oppressed. Her own assessment perhaps sums up her life best of all: 'I have never deserted a cause in its days of hardship and adversity.'[70]

Conclusion

Sylvia Pankhurst's wide-ranging contribution to British and radical politics has been frequently overlooked; only a few of her campaigning efforts are well known. This has deprived us of an understanding of how, while adopting seemingly different causes, these campaigns fitted into the wider struggle she was waging: the right for people to determine their own lives in a more directly democratic system. Beyond the direct campaigns she has been overlooked in other spheres too. For most of her life Sylvia Pankhurst edited a radical weekly newspaper that appeared under conditions of censorship and during her imprisonments, and survived police raids. She commissioned leading journalists from around the world and used her paper to give voice to the marginalised and oppressed – those who would otherwise not have been heard. It is not only the fact that she was a woman newspaper editor that makes her an outstanding figure, it is also the fact that her newspapers were impressive examples of investigative journalism. Yet there is no study of Sylvia's contribution to journalism.

As a socialist she drew on an eclectic range of ideas – sometimes the ethical socialism from her youth, sometimes the scientific socialism of Marxism, as well as abstentionist ideas in the early 1920s. She was not and never claimed to be a socialist theorist, but some conclusions can be drawn about her contribution to the socialist movement.

She was undoubtedly, as Mary Davis has argued, a 'voluntarist' – believing that political will was all that was needed to overcome all material circumstances.[1] She probably developed this approach in the suffragette movement, not only because the suffragettes proved that acts of militancy could force women's suffrage into the limelight, but also because she proved the WSPU leadership wrong. While they felt that an effective militant movement could not be built by working-class women, the ELFS proved not only that it could but that they could be more radical, organise in greater numbers, and through these tactics achieve a more significant development than the WSPU. It was the ELFS that won an audience with Asquith and his commitment to a more democratic franchise measure.

But perhaps Sylvia too closely associated the ELFS's success with her own political development. While it is true that it was her decision to break with WSPU tactics that led to the development of a new kind of working-class militancy, it is also difficult to see how the same thing could have been achieved had she not made this break at the height of the industrial unrest which was particularly acute around the East London docks. Her radical ideas resonated with workers taking militant action of their own.

When the working-class movement found itself in retreat after the 1919 unrest she blamed the subjective influence of ideas about reforming the system and not the objective circumstances of rising unemployment. In defining the problem as subjective, Sylvia sought subjective solutions, concluding that she needed to be more revolutionary and more detached from the parties of reform to counter the influence of reformist ideas, a position that left her isolated from the working-class movement.

However, she never allowed her voluntarist approach to lead her to believe that change came solely through individuals. She was committed to the idea that socialism could only come from below. In the first few decades of her life she put this into practice most spectacularly by building mass movements. She built an effective working-class suffragette movement which inspired community resistance to police brutality. She also built an influential organisation in East London at the forefront of radical, political developments to the extent that it even declared itself the first British Communist Party. When she became isolated from British movements she nevertheless remained committed to the principle of self-determination, and through her internationalism she became a leading and profound critic of imperialism able to relate to, and practically assist, the emerging anti-colonialist movement. This is why Sylvia Pankhurst is important. Though she did not always pursue the most effective strategies, throughout her life she helped ordinary people to speak for themselves – which was what she ultimately always aimed to do.

Notes

INTRODUCTION

1. E.S. Pankhurst, *The Suffragette: The History of the Women's Militant Suffrage Movement 1905–10* (London: Gay & Hancock Limited, 1911), p. 44.
2. E.S. Pankhurst, *The Suffragette Movement: An Intimate Account of Persons and Ideals* (London: Virago Limited, 1977), pp. 193–4.
3. Pankhurst, *The Suffragette*, p. 46

CHAPTER 1

1. S. Pankhurst, in Countess of Oxford and Asquith (ed.), *Myself When Young: By Famous Women of To-Day* (London: Frederick Muller Ltd., 1938), p. 259.
2. Quoted in C. Pankhurst, *Unshackled: The Story of How We Won the Vote* (London: Hutchinson & Co. Ltd., 1959), p. 22.
3. For example, *Manchester Guardian*, 24 September 1883.
4. For example, *Manchester Guardian*, 28 September 1883.
5. See *Manchester Examiner and Times*, 23 October 1883, in the Estelle Sylvia Pankhurst Papers at the Internationaal Instituut Voor Sociale Geschiedenis, Amsterdam (henceforward 'ESP Papers'), and Pankhurst, *The Suffragette Movement*, p. 65.
6. L. Raw, *Striking a Light: The Bryant and May Matchwomen and their Place in History* (London: Continuum, 2011), p. 168.
7. Pankhurst, *Myself When Young*, p. 265.
8. Pankhurst, *The Suffragette Movement*, p. 67.
9. Ibid.
10. Pankhurst, *Myself When Young*, p. 262.
11. Pankhurst, *The Suffragette Movement*, p. 67.
12. Pankhurst, *Myself When Young*, p. 267; see also R. Pankhurst, *Sylvia Pankhurst: Artist and Crusader* (New York and London: Paddington Press Ltd., 1979), p. 21.
13. Pankhurst, *Myself When Young*, p. 267.
14. Mrs Pankhurst quoted in *The Labour Leader*, 4 July 1896, p. 230.
15. Pankhurst, *The Suffragette Movement*, p. 90.
16. Quoted in *Women's Franchise League Report of Proceedings at the Inaugural Meeting* (London: The Hansard Publishing Union Limited, n.d. [1889]), p. 19.

17. Ibid., pp. 25, 26.
18. Ibid., pp. 15–16.
19. Programme of the Women's Franchise League International Conference, p. 1, ESP Papers.
20. See also T. Cliff and D. Gluckstein, *The Labour Party: A Marxist History* (London: Bookmarks Publications Ltd., 1996), p. 11.
21. *I.L.P. News*, April 1898, p. 7.
22. Ibid.
23. Pankhurst, *The Suffragette Movement*, p. 129.
24. Ibid., p. 135.
25. Ibid., p. 126.
26. Ibid., p. 123.
27. *The Labour Leader*, 11 July 1896, p. 235.
28. Pankhurst, *The Suffragette Movement*, p. 151.
29. Ibid., pp. 154–5.
30. Ibid., p. 155.
31. Ibid., p. 156.
32. Ibid., pp. 155–6.
33. Ibid., p. 162.
34. J. Dunham, Amy K. Browning (1881–1978): An Impressionist in the Women's Movement (Saxmundham: Boudicca Books, 1995), p. 6.
35. Pankhurst, *The Suffragette Movement*, p. 171.

CHAPTER 2

1. J. Liddington and J. Norris, *One Hand Tied Behind Us: The Rise of the Women's Suffrage Movement* (London: Virago Press, 1978), p. 27.
2. *I.L.P. News*, August 1903, p. 1.
3. Pankhurst, *The Suffragette Movement*, p. 167.
4. T. Billington-Greig, 'The birth of the Women's Freedom League', in C. McPhee and A. FitzGerald (eds), *The Non-Violent Militant: Selected Writings of Teresa Billington-Greig* (London: Routledge & Kegan Paul), p. 103.
5. See A. Kenney, *Memories of a Militant* (London: E. Arnold & Co., 1924), p. 27.
6. McPhee and FitzGerald, *The Non-Violent Militant*, p. 4.
7. Kenney, *Memories of a Militant*, p. 30.
8. Pankhurst, *The Suffragette Movement*, pp. 184–5; C. Pankhurst, *Unshackled*, p. 48.
9. E. Pethick-Lawrence, *My Part in a Changing World* (London: Victor Gollancz, 1938), p. 148.
10. Pankhurst, *The Suffragette Movement*, p. 197.
11. Pankhurst, *The Suffragette*, p. 57.
12. Ibid., p. 72.

13. Kenney, *Memories of a Militant*, p. 69.

14. Ibid., p. 70; Pankhurst, *The Suffragette*, p. 57.

15. Minutes of 27 February 1906, in Minute Book of Canning Town W.S.P.U Branch, 1906–7, Museum of London, 50 82/1133.

16. Minute Book of Canning Town W.S.P.U Branch, 1906–7, Museum of London, 50 82/1133.

17. Kenney, *Memories of a Militant*, p. 59.

18. WSPU leaflet, Minnie Baldock Papers, Museum of London, 60/15/13.

19. The similarity is also noted in Pankhurst, *Sylvia Pankhurst: Artist and Crusader*, p. 62; J. Duckworth, 'Sylvia Pankhurst as an artist', in I. Bullock and R. Pankhurst, *Sylvia Pankhurst: From Artist to Anti-Fascist* (London: Macmillan, 1992), p. 43.

20. Pankhurst, *The Suffragette Movement*, p. 212.

21. Ibid.

22. On this see K. Cowman, *Women of the Right Spirit: Paid Organisers of the Women's Social and Political Union (WSPU) 1904–18* (Manchester: Manchester University Press, 2007), p. 12.

23. Pankhurst, *The Suffragette Movement*, pp. 197, 205.

24. Ibid., p. 215.

25. M. Bondfield, *A Life's Work* (London: Hutchinson & Co. Ltd, 1948), pp. 81–5.

26. Quoted in P. Foot, *The Vote: How It was Won and How It was Undermined* (London: Viking, 2005), p. 204.

27. On the 'statistically useless' survey, see L. Garner, 'Suffragism and Socialism: Sylvia Pankhurst 1903–1914', in Bullock and Pankhurst, *Sylvia Pankhurst*, p. 62.

28. Pankhurst, *The Suffragette Movement*, p. 248.

29. Ibid., p. 203.

30. Pankhurst, *The Suffragette Movement*, p. 269.

31. *The Bury & Norwich Post & Suffolk Standard*, 20 August 1907, pp. 5, 7.

32. Pankhurst, *The Suffragette Movement*, pp. 269–70.

33. Ibid., p. 241.

34. Ibid.

35. Correspondence quoted in M. Pugh, *The Pankhursts* (London: Allen Lane, 2001), p. 169.

36. Pethick-Lawrence, *My Part in a Changing World*, pp. 174–5; on the trade union-style structure of local branches see Pankhurst, *The Suffragette Movement*, p. 266.

37. Billington-Greig, 'The birth of the Women's Freedom League', p. 103.

38. Pankhurst, *The Suffragette Movement*, p. 264.

39. Pethick-Lawrence, *My Part in a Changing World*, p. 176.

40. Pankhurst, *Unshackled*, p. 82.

41. E. Smyth, 'The March of the Women' (lyrics by C. Hamilton), in G. Norquay (ed.), *Voices & Votes: A Literary Anthology of the Women's*

Suffrage Campaign (Manchester: Manchester University Press, 1995), p. 94.

42. Pankhurst, *The Suffragette Movement*, p. 265.
43. *Votes for Women*, October 1907, p. 6.
44. C. Pankhurst, *The Militant Methods of the N.W.S.P.U* (London: The Woman's Press, 1908), p. 13.
45. See for example E. Pankhurst, *The Importance of the Vote* (London: The Woman's Press, 1908), pp. 4–5.
46. *Votes for Women*, 9 July 1908, p. 296.
47. Minutes of 19 March 1907, 26 March 1907, 3 December 1907, in Minute Book of Canning Town W.S.P.U Branch, 1906–7, Museum of London, 50 82/1133.
48. Pankhurst, *The Suffragette Movement*, pp. 230–7.
49. Ibid., p. 238.
50. Ibid.
51. Quoted in B. Winslow, *Sylvia Pankhurst: Sexual Politics and Political Activism* (London: UCL Press, 1996), p. 24.
52. *Votes for Women*, 26 August 1910, p. 776.
53. S. Pankhurst, 'The potato-pickers', *Votes for Women*, 28 January 1909, p. 294.
54. In this I disagree with the fascinating chapter on Sylvia's writing on work by Morag Shiach, in which she locates Sylvia's depiction of the potato women as physically horrifying in a distinction made by Sylvia between self-respecting and degenerate poor. This would indeed be uncharacteristic of Sylvia and I believe the main difference in her presentation between these workers and others she portrays more positively is their relative equality with male workers, a theme that clearly relates to Sylvia's concerns at the time. See M. Shiach, *Modernism, Labour and Selfhood in British Literature and Culture, 1890–1930* (Cambridge: Cambridge University Press, 2004), Chapter 3.
55. *Votes for Women*, 26 August 1910, p. 776.
56. Ibid.
57. *Votes for Women*, 11 August 1911, p. 730.
58. Pankhurst, *The Suffragette Movement*, p. 278.
59. Ibid., p. 285.
60. Ibid., p. 286.
61. *Votes for Women*, 9 July 1908, p. 297.
62. *Votes for Women*, 25 June 1908, p. 265.
63. *Votes for Women*, 9 July 1908, p. 298.
64. *Votes for Women*, 2 July 1908, p. 280.
65. A. Raeburn, *The Militant Suffragettes* (London: Michael Joseph, 1973), p. 134.
66. C. Lytton and J. Warton, *Prisons and Prisoners: Some Personal Experiences* (London: Virago Press, 1988), p. 235.
67. See J. Liddington, *Rebel Girls: Their Fight for the Vote* (London: Virago Press, 2006), pp. 97–103.

68. Pankhurst, *The Suffragette Movement*, p. 215.
69. For a related point see Winslow, *Sylvia Pankhurst*, p. 19.

CHAPTER 3

1. Pankhurst, *The Suffragette Movement*, p. 347.
2. J.K. Hardie to E.S. Pankhurst, 10 March 1911, ESP Papers.
3. Pankhurst, 'Chronicle of two visits', pp. 8–9, ESP papers.
4. For Sylvia's movements on the trip see Pankhurst, *The Suffragette Movement*, pp. 147–8; *Votes for Women*, 27 January 1911, p. 278, 10 February 1911, p. 304, 14 April 1911, p. 462, 21 April 1911, p. 472.
5. *Chicago Sunday Tribune* quoted in *Votes for Women*, 10 February 1911, p. 304.
6. Quoted in *Votes for Women*, 14 April 1911, p. 462.
7. *Votes for Women*, 21 April 1911, p. 472.
8. *Votes for Women*, 14 April 1911, p. 462, 21 April 1911, p. 472.
9. Pankhurst, 'Chronicle of two visits', p. 5.
10. Ibid., p. 3.
11. Ibid., p. 7.
12. See H. Zinn, *A People's History of the United States: 1492–Present* (Harlow: Pearson Education Limited, 2003), pp. 326–7.
13. Pankhurst, 'Chronicle of two visits', p. 3.
14. *Votes for Women*, 16 February 1912, p. 305.
15. E.S. Pankhurst to J.K. Hardie [n.d.], ESP Papers.
16. Pankhurst, 'Chronicle of two visits', pp. 2–7.
17. Ibid., p. 3.
18. Ibid., p. 36.
19. Pankhurst, *The Suffragette Movement*, p. 348.
20. Pankhurst, 'Chronicle of two visits', p. 12.
21. *The Suffragette*, 21 November 1913, p. 124.
22. E.S. Pankhurst to J.K. Hardie, 5 February 1912, ESP Papers.
23. L. Garner, 'Suffragism and Socialism: Sylvia Pankhurst 1903–1914', in Bullock and Pankhurst, *Sylvia Pankhurst*, p. 71.
24. *Votes for Women*, 25 August 1911, p. 754.
25. *Votes for Women*, 18 August 1911, p. 742.
26. U. de la Mare, 'Necessity and rage: the factory women's strikes in Bermondsey, 1911', *History Workshop Journal*, 66 (2008), p. 73.
27. Ibid., p. 69.
28. Ibid., p. 73.
29. *Daily Chronicle* quoted in M.A. Hamilton, *Mary Macarthur: A Biographical Sketch* (London: Leonard Parsons Ltd., 1925), p. 105.
30. de la Mare, 'Necessity and rage', pp. 74, 75, 77; Hamilton, *Mary Macarthur*, p. 106.
31. *Votes for Women*, 18 August 1911, p. 742.

32. *Votes for Women*, 11 October 1912, p. 26.
33. *Votes for Women*, 6 October 1911, p. 4.
34. Pankhurst, *The Suffragette Movement*, p. 372.
35. Pankhurst, *Unshackled*, p. 202.
36. Pankhurst, *The Suffragette Movement*, p. 384.
37. *Votes for Women*, 14 June 1912, p. 597.
38. *Votes for Women*, 21 June 1912, p. 620.
39. Ibid.
40. Pankhurst, *The Suffragette Movement*, p. 416.
41. Ibid., p. 417.
42. *East London Observer*, 12 October 1912, p. 7.
43. *The Suffragette*, 25 October 1912, p. 24.
44. Pankhurst, *The Suffragette Movement*, p. 419.
45. *The Suffragette*, 18 October 1912, p. 9.
46. Ibid.
47. *The Suffragette*, 1 November 1912, p. 40.
48. *The Suffragette*, 25 October 1912, p. 24.
49. K. Harding and C. Gibbs, 'Interview with Annie Barnes', in V. Murray, *Echoes of the East End* (London: Viking, 1989), p. 48.
50. B. Harrison interview with Miss Elsie Lagsding, 15 June 1976, Women's Library Recordings, 8SUF/B/094, Women's Library, London Metropolitan University.
51. Pankhurst, *The Suffragette Movement*, p. 524.
52. B. Harrison interview with Mrs Elsie Flint, 19 December 1974, Women's Library Recordings, 8SUF/B/029, Women's Library, London Metropolitan University.
53. *The Suffragette*, 18 October 1912, p. 7.
54. *Votes for Women*, 11 October 1912, p. 24.
55. M. Pugh, *March of the Women: A Revisionist Analysis of the Campaign for Women's Suffrage, 1866–1914* (Oxford: Oxford University Press, 2002), p. 269.
56. *The Suffragette*, 18 October 1913, p. 7.
57. J. Purvis, *Emmeline Pankhurst* (London: Routledge, 2002), p. 109; P. Bartley, *Emmeline Pankhurst* (London: Routledge, 2002), p. 136.
58. Liddington, *Rebel Girls*, pp. 226–7; Pankhurst, *The Suffragette Movement*, p. 406.
59. *The Suffragette*, 20 December 1912, p. 141.
60. E.S. Pankhurst, 'The women's movement of yesterday and tomorrow', unpublished typescript, n.d., ESP Papers.
61. Pankhurst, *The Suffragette Movement*, p. 441.
62. Harrison interview with Miss Elsie Lagsding.
63. Pankhurst, *The Suffragette Movement*, pp. 443–4.
64. *The Suffragette*, 28 March 1913, p. 385.
65. Pankhurst, *The Suffragette Movement*, p. 444.
66. *The Suffragette*, 21 March 1913, p. 364.

67. Ibid.
68. Pankhurst, *The Suffragette Movement*, p. 448.
69. Ibid., p. 450.
70. Ibid., p. 491.
71. Ibid., p. 509.
72. Harrison interview with Miss Elsie Lagsding.
73. Pankhurst, *The Suffragette Movement*, p. 509.
74. See *Woman's Dreadnought*, 21 March 1914, p. 3.
75. E.S. Pankhurst to Captain White, undated, ESP Papers.
76. Pankhurst, *The Suffragette Movement*, p. 500.
77. See J. Newsinger, *Rebel City: Larkin, Connolly and the Dublin Labour Movement* (London: The Merlin Press Ltd., 2004), p. viii.
78. *Daily Herald*, 3 November 1913, p. 7.
79. *The Freeman's Journal*, 3 November 1913, p. 7.
80. *Daily Herald*, 3 November 1913, p. 7.
81. Ibid.
82. Ibid.
83. Pankhurst, *The Suffragette Movement*, p. 502.
84. Ibid., p. 516.
85. Ibid., p. 518.
86. Ibid.
87. Quoted in Pugh, *The Pankhursts*, p. 286.
88. Pankhurst, *The Suffragette Movement*, p. 517.
89. Minute book of the East London Federation of the Suffragettes, 27 January 1914, ESP Papers.
90. Ibid.
91. Pankhurst, *The Suffragette Movement*, p. 542.
92. *Woman's Dreadnought*, 6 June 1914, p. 46.
93. C. Pankhurst, *The Great Scourge and How to End It* (London: E. Pankhurst, 1913), p. ix.
94. Ibid., p. 17.
95. *Woman's Dreadnought*, 8 March 1914, p. 5.
96. C. Pankhurst, *The Great Scourge*, p. vii.
97. *Woman's Dreadnought*, 8 March 1914, p. 3.
98. *Woman's Dreadnought*, 8 March 1914, p. 1; Pankhurst, *The Suffragette Movement*, p. 525.
99. Pankhurst, *The Suffragette Movement*, p. 526.
100. Ibid., pp. 525–6.
101. *Woman's Dreadnought*, 28 March 1914, p. 3, and 21 March 1914, p. 3.
102. *Woman's Dreadnought*, 28 March 1914, p. 3, and 25 April 1914, p. 1.
103. *Woman's Dreadnought*, 23 May 1914, p. 39.
104. *Woman's Dreadnought*, 18 April 1914, p. 3.
105. *Woman's Dreadnought*, 18 July 1914, p. 72; R. Taylor, *In Letters of Gold: The Story of Sylvia Pankhurst and the East London Federation of the*

Suffragettes in Bow (London: Stepney Books, 1993), p. 21; Pankhurst, *The Suffragette Movement*, pp. 542–3.

106. *Woman's Dreadnought*, 18 July 1914, p. 72, and 25 July 1914, p. 73.
107. Pankhurst, *The Suffragette Movement*, p. 543.
108. *Woman's Dreadnought*, 30 April 1914, p. 44.
109. For example, *Woman's Dreadnought*, 21 March 1914, p. 2.
110. Pankhurst, *The Suffragette Movement*, p. 565.
111. Ibid., p. 571.
112. Ibid., p. 572.
113. *Woman's Dreadnought*, 27 June 1914, p. 59.
114. Ibid.
115. Ibid., p. 60.

CHAPTER 4

1. *Woman's Dreadnought*, 1 August 1914.
2. E.S. Pankhurst, *The Home Front: A Mirror to Life in England During the First World War* (London: The Cresset Library, 1987), p. 12.
3. J. Liddington, *The Long Road to Greenham: Feminism and Anti-Militarism in Britain since 1820* (London: Virago Press, 1989), p. 74.
4. Quoted in H.M. Swanwick, *I Have Been Young* (London: Victor Gollancz Ltd., 1935), p. 240; A. Wiltsher, *Most Dangerous Women: Feminist Peace Campaigners of the Great War* (London: Pandora Press, 1985), p. 23.
5. G. Radice and L. Radice, *Will Thorne: Constructive Militant. A Study in New Unionism and New Politics* (London: George Allen & Unwin Ltd., 1974), p. 72.
6. Quoted in J. Vellacott, *Pacifists, Patriots and the Vote: The Erosion of Democratic Suffragism in Britain during the First World War* (Basingstoke: Palgrave-Macmillan, 2007), p. 76.
7. *Workers' Dreadnought*, 17 April 1920, p. 1.
8. Pankhurst, *The Home Front*, p. 16.
9. B. Harrison interviews with Mrs Elsie Flint; Miss Elsie Lagsding; Miss Jessie Stephen, 8SUF/B/157, 1 July 1977, Women's Library Recordings.
10. ELFS Minute Book, 6 August 1914 [n.p].
11. Ibid.
12. For example, *Woman's Dreadnought*, 1 August 1914, p. 78.
13. ELFS Minute Book, 6 August 1914.
14. Pankhurst, *The Home Front*, p. 29.
15. *Woman's Dreadnought*, 15 August 1914, p. 85.
16. Pankhurst, *The Home Front*, p. 217.
17. Minutes of ELFS General Meeting, 9 August 1915, ESP Papers.
18. *Woman's Dreadnought*, 18 September 1915, p. 319.
19. J. Bush, *Behind the Lines: East London Labour 1914–1919* (London: The Merlin Press, 1984), p. 37.

20. *Woman's Dreadnought*, 15 August 1914, p. 85.
21. *Woman's Dreadnought*, 15 May 1915, p. 246.
22. East London Federation of the Suffragettes, *First Annual Report* (London: 400 Old Ford Road, Bow, E., 1915), p. 17.
23. Pankhurst, *The Home Front*, p. 212.
24. See ibid., pp. 242–4.
25. ELFS, *First Annual Report*, p. 17.
26. Pankhurst, *The Home Front*, p. 85.
27. Ibid., p. 22.
28. Ibid.
29. Ibid., p. 43.
30. Ibid.
31. Harrison interview with Miss Elsie Lagsding.
32. Pankhurst, *The Home Front*, p. 22.
33. Ibid., p. 72.
34. Ibid.
35. ELFS, *First Annual Report*, p. 18.
36. Pankhurst, *The Home Front*, p. 22, see also p. 73.
37. Ibid., p. 399; Harrison interview with Mrs Elsie Flint.
38. Pankhurst, *The Home Front*, pp. 333–5.
39. Ibid., p. 286.
40. Ibid., p. 28.
41. *Woman's Dreadnought*, 12 December 1914, p. 155.
42. *Woman's Dreadnought*, 25 September 1915, p. 325.
43. *Woman's Dreadnought*, 3 November 1917, p. 875.
44. Pankhurst, *The Home Front*, p. 205.
45. *Woman's Dreadnought*, 10 July 1915, p. 277.
46. Winslow, *Sylvia Pankhurst*, p. 99.
47. A. Marwick, *The Deluge: British Society and the First World War* (London and Hampshire: Macmillan Education Ltd., 1991), p. 116.
48. Pankhurst, *The Home Front*, p. 221.
49. Ibid., p. 222.
50. Minutes of the Council of the ELFS, 19 July 1915, ESP Papers.
51. On Rose Pengelly see Pankhurst, *The Home Front*, p. 20.
52. See C.A. Culleton, *Working-Class Culture, Women, and Britain, 1914–1921* (New York: St. Martin's Press, 1999), p. 39.
53. Ibid., p. 34.
54. M. Craig, *When the Clyde Ran Red* (Edinburgh: Mainstream Publishing Company, 2011), p. 110.
55. Ibid., p. 113.
56. Pankhurst, *The Home Front*, p. 262.
57. Ibid., p. 202.
58. *Woman's Dreadnought*, 2 October 1915, p. 330.
59. *Woman's Dreadnought*, 15 July 1916, p. 511, and 5 August 1916, p. 523.
60. Minutes of the Council of the ELFS, 16 April 1917, ESP Papers.

61. Pankhurst, *The Home Front*, p. 52.
62. *Woman's Dreadnought*, 3 October 1914, p. 115.
63. *Woman's Dreadnought*, 21 October 1916, p. 576, and 28 October 1916, p. 577; see also S.L. Bird, *Stepney: Profile of a London Borough from the Outbreak of the First World War to the Festival of Britain, 1914–1951* (Newcastle upon Tyne: Cambridge Scholars Publishing, 2011), p. 40.
64. ELFS Minutes of General Meetings, 17 January 1916, ESP Papers.
65. Vellacott, *Pacifists, Patriots and the Vote*, p. 133.
66. M. Arncliffe Sennett, *The Child* (London: C.W. Daniel Company Limited, 1938), p. 120.
67. Pankhurst, *The Home Front*, p. 153; Wiltsher, *Most Dangerous Women*, p. 133.
68. Pankhurst, *The Home Front*, p. 69.
69. *Woman's Dreadnought*, 8 April 1916, p. 456.
70. Pankhurst, *The Home Front*, p. 225.
71. Quoted in Pankhurst, *The Home Front*, p. 235.
72. Pankhurst, *The Home Front*, p. 230.
73. L. German, *How a Century of War Changed the Lives of Women* (London: Pluto Press, 2013), p. 23.
74. *Woman's Dreadnought*, 25 March 1916, p. 448.
75. Pankhurst, *The Home Front*, p. 322.
76. Ibid., p. 417.
77. Swanwick, *I Have Been Young*, p. 188.
78. Harrison interview with Miss Elsie Lagsding.

CHAPTER 5

1. L. Trotsky, *The History of the Russian Revolution*, trans. M. Eastman (London: Pluto Press, 1997), p. 122.
2. Ibid., pp. 122–3.
3. D. Gluckstein, *The Western Soviets: Workers' Councils Versus Parliament 1915–1920* (London: Bookmarks, 1985), p. 20.
4. Ibid., p. 21.
5. *Woman's Dreadnought*, 24 March 1917, p. 704.
6. W. Kendall, *The Revolutionary Movement in Britain 1900–21: The Origins of British Communism* (London: Weidenfeld and Nicolson, 1969), p. 170.
7. Ibid., p. 124; *Woman's Dreadnought*, 24 March 1917, p. 704.
8. E.S. Pankhurst, *Execution of an East London Boy* (London: Workers' Suffrage Federation, n.d.).
9. Pankhurst, *The Home Front*, p. 291.
10. Ibid., p. 371.
11. *Woman's Dreadnought*, 10 February 1917, p. 671.
12. *Woman's Dreadnought*, 31 March 1917, p. 712.

13. Ibid.

14. Ibid.

15. *Woman's Dreadnought*, 26 May 1917, p. 760.

16. *Woman's Dreadnought*, 3 March 1917, p. 688, my emphasis.

17. Quoted in I. Bullock, 'Sylvia Pankhurst and the Russian Revolution: the making of a "left wing" communist', in Bullock and Pankhurst, *Sylvia Pankhurst*, p. 129.

18. *East End News*, 20 March 1917, cutting in Tower Hamlets Local History Archive.

19. *Workers' Dreadnought*, 21 February 1920, p. 4.

20. *Woman's Dreadnought*, 24 March 1917, p. 705.

21. E.S. Pankhurst, 'When I sat with the present Prime Minister on the Workers' and Soldiers' Council of Great Britain', unpublished typescript [n.d.], p. 5, ESP Papers.

22. Ibid., p. 6.

23. *Woman's Dreadnought*, 9 June 1917, p. 773.

24. Pankhurst, 'When I sat with the present Prime Minister', p. 15.

25. *Workers' Dreadnought*, 17 November 1917, p. 884.

26. *Workers' Dreadnought*, 6 July 1918, p. 1031.

27. E.S. Pankhurst, 'In the red twilight', unpublished MS, p. vii, ESP Papers.

28. Ibid.

29. Pankhurst, 'In the red twilight', p. 148.

30. H. Pollitt, *Serving My Time: An Apprenticeship to Politics* (London: Lawrence and Wishart, 1950), p. 112.

31. W.F. Watson, *Watson's Reply* (London, 1920), p. 18.

32. Pankhurst, 'In the red twilight', p. 19.

33. Pollitt, *Serving My Time*, p. 112.

34. Ibid., p. 114.

35. *Workers' Dreadnought*, 15 May 1920, p. 4.

36. For days lost see C. Rosenberg, *1919: Britain on the Brink of Revolution* (London: Bookmarks, 1987), p. 11.

37. Quoted in Kendall, *The Revolutionary Movement in Britain*, p. 168.

38. Rosenberg, *1919*, p. 11.

39. L. German and J. Rees, *A People's History of London* (London: Verso, 2012), p. 185.

40. Rosenberg, *1919*, p. 36.

41. Kendall, *The Revolutionary Movement in Britain*, pp. 203–4.

42. V.I. Lenin, *Lenin On Britain* (London: Lawrence and Wishart, 1973) p. 362.

43. Ibid., p. 363.

44. Ibid., p. 365.

45. C. Harman, *The Lost Revolution: Germany 1918–23* (London: Bookmarks, 1997), p. 82.

46. Minute Book of the WSF, 27 September 1918, p. 10, ESP Papers.

47. Pankhurst, 'In the red twilight', p. 128.

48. In V.I. Lenin, *The Emancipation of Women: From the Writings of V.I. Lenin* (New York: International Publishers, 1984), p. 60.
49. *Workers' Dreadnought*, 16 February 1918, p. 948.
50. Winslow, *Sylvia Pankhurst*, pp. 151–3.
51. Pankhurst, 'In the red twilight', p. 27.
52. Ibid., p. 31.
53. Winslow, *Sylvia Pankhurst*, p. 141; Harrison interview with Elsie Lagsding; Pankhurst, 'In the red twilight', p. 129.
54. *Workers' Dreadnought*, 13 December 1919, p. 1570.
55. See Kendall, *The Revolutionary Movement in Britain*, p. 207.
56. Winslow, *Sylvia Pankhurst*, pp. 164–5.
57. E.S. Pankhurst, *Soviet Russia As I Saw It* (London: The Dreadnought Publishers, 1921), p. 8.
58. *Workers' Dreadnought*, 21 February 1920, p. 6.
59. Ibid., pp. 5, 6.
60. V.I. Lenin, *'Left-Wing' Communism: An Infantile Disorder* (London: Bookmarks, 1993), p. 116.
61. J. Riddell (ed.), *Workers of the World and Oppressed Peoples, Unite!: Proceedings and Documents of the Second Congress 1920*, Vol. II (New York: Pathfinder Press, 1991), p. 739.
62. Lenin, *'Left-Wing' Communism*, p. 109.
63. Riddell, *Workers of the World*, p. 744; Pankhurst, *Soviet Russia As I Saw It*, p. 52.
64. J.T. Murphy, *New Horizons* (London: Bodley Head, 1941), p. 151.
65. Pankhurst, *Soviet Russia As I Saw It*, p. 46.
66. Kendall, *The Revolutionary Movement in Britain*, pp. 258.
67. *Woman's Dreadnought*, 26 May 1917, pp. 758, 760.
68. C. McKay, *A Long Way From Home* (London and Sydney: Pluto Press, 1985), p. 68.
69. P. Fryer, *Staying Power: The History of Black People in Britain* (London: Pluto Press, 1984), pp. 298–9.
70. Ibid., pp. 299–310.
71. 'Appeal of Miss Sylvia Pankhurst against sentence of six months imprisonment [...] for articles in the *Workers' Dreadnought*', October 1920, pp. 16–17, ESP Papers.
72. *Workers' Dreadnought*, 7 June 1919, p. 1354.
73. McKay, *A Long Way From Home*, p. 75.
74. *Workers' Dreadnought*, 24 April 1920, p. 2.
75. Fryer, *Staying Power*, p. 318.
76. McKay, *A Long Way From Home*, p. 76.
77. *Workers' Dreadnought*, 16 October 1920, p. 3.
78. *Workers' Dreadnought*, 6 November 1920, p. 1.
79. Ibid.
80. Ibid.
81. Kendall, *The Revolutionary Movement in Britain*, pp. 266–7.

82. *Workers' Dreadnought*, 4 June 1921, p. 8.
83. N. Branson, *Poplarism, 1919–1925: George Lansbury and the Councillors' Revolt* (London: Lawrence and Wishart, 1980), p. 29.
84. *Workers' Dreadnought*, 10 September 1921, p. 4.

CHAPTER 6

1. Quoted in T. Behan, *The Resistible Rise of Benito Mussolini* (London: Bookmarks, 2003), p. 32.
2. Ibid., p. 41.
3. Quoted in ibid., p. 113.
4. *Workers' Dreadnought*, 11 November 1922, p. 1.
5. J.R. Walkowitz, *Nights Out: Life in Cosmopolitan London* (New Haven and London: Yale University Press, 2012), p. 112.
6. Ibid., p. 129.
7. Ibid., pp. 121–2; L. Sponza, *Divided Loyalties: Italians in Britain during the Second World War* (Bern: Peter Lang, 2000), p. 32.
8. Richard Pankhurst, interview with the author, 2 August 2012.
9. D. Sassoon, *Mussolini and the Rise of Fascism* (London: HarperCollins, 2007), p. 141.
10. K. Hodgson, *Fighting Fascism: The British Left and the Rise of Fascism, 1919–39* (Manchester: Manchester University Press, 2010), p. 52.
11. *Workers' Dreadnought*, 11 November 1922, p. 1.
12. *Workers' Dreadnought*, 14 April 1923, p. 1.
13. Quoted in *Workers' Dreadnought*, 4 November 1922, p. 1.
14. *Workers' Dreadnought*, 11 November 1922, p. 1.
15. *Workers' Dreadnought*, 17 March 1923, p. 8.
16. R. Pankhurst, 'Sylvia Pankhurst and the Italian anti-fascist movement: the Women's International Matteotti Committee', *Socialist History*, 19 (2001), 17–19.
17. *Workers' Dreadnought*, 4 November 1922, p. 4.
18. Quoted in Behan, *The Resistible Rise*, p. 92.
19. Sponza, *Divided Loyalties*, p. 37; Walkowitz, *Nights Out*, p. 112.
20. *New Times and Ethiopia News*, 10 October 1936, p. 6.
21. Sponza, *Divided Loyalties*, p. 37, n. 40.
22. Riddell, *Proceedings*, Vol. 1, p. 233.
23. Ibid., p. 231.
24. Ibid., p. 221.
25. *Workers' Dreadnought*, 24 July 1920, p. 4.
26. E.S. Pankhurst, *India and the Earthly Paradise* (Bombay: Sunshine Publishing House, 1926).
27. S. Harrison, *Sylvia Pankhurst: A Crusading Life 1882–1960* (London: Aurum Press Ltd., 2003), p. 219; Pugh, *The Pankhursts*, p. 400.
28. Thanks to Jane Mackelworth for drawing my attention to this.

29. Pankhurst, *India and the Earthly Paradise*, pp. 163–4.
30. Ibid., pp. 171–2.
31. Purvis, *Emmeline Pankhurst*, p. 327.
32. Harrison, *Sylvia Pankhurst*, p. 220.
33. For example, see Purvis, *Emmeline Pankhurst*, p. 350.
34. E.S. Pankhurst, *Save the Mothers* (London: Alfred A. Knopf, 1930), p. 36.
35. Ibid., pp. 108–9.
36. Ibid., p. 109.
37. Ibid., p. 110.
38. Ibid., p. 121.
39. Ibid., pp. 132–4.
40. Pankhurst, *Myself When Young*, p. 311.
41. 'Fascism As It Is', in K. Dodd (ed.), *A Sylvia Pankhurst Reader* (Manchester: Manchester University Press, 1993), p. 227.
42. R. Pankhurst, 'Sylvia Pankhurst and the Italian anti-fascist movement', pp. 3, 5.
43. Ibid., pp. 3, 4, 22.
44. R. Pankhurst, *Sylvia Pankhurst: Artist and Crusader*, p. 209.
45. Harrison, *Sylvia Pankhurst*, p. 215; Pugh, *The Pankhursts*, p. 420.
46. Quoted in R. Pankhurst, *Sylvia Pankhurst: Counsel for Ethiopia* (Hollywood: Tsehai Publishers, 2003), p. 17.
47. *Birmingham Gazette*, 13 November 1935, newspaper cutting in Women's Library, 7ESP/01 2002/27.

CHAPTER 7

1. B. Winslow, 'The first white Rastafarian: Sylvia Pankhurst, Haile Selassie, and Ethiopia', in R. Hackett, F. Hauser and G. Wachman (eds), *At Home and Abroad in the Empire: British Women Write the 1930s* (Newark: University of Delaware Press, 2009), p. 179.
2. R. Pankhurst, *The Ethiopians* (Oxford: Blackwell, 1998), p. 219.
3. Ibid., p. 223.
4. J. Dugan and L. Lafore, *Days of Emperor and Clown: The Italo-Ethiopian War 1935–1936* (New York: Doubleday & Company, 1973), p. 107.
5. Quoted in R. Pankhurst, *The Ethiopians*, p. 224.
6. Dugan and Lafore, *Days of Emperor and Clown*, p. 184.
7. R. Pankhurst, *The Ethiopians*, p. 230.
8. A point Sylvia made at the time; see *New Times and Ethiopia News* (henceforward *NTEN*), 31 October 1953, p. 4.
9. E.S. Pankhurst, letter to *Daily Herald*, 3 October 1935, quoted in *NTEN*, 7 November 1953, p. 4.
10. See for example Sylvia's letters to the press from 1935, quoted in *NTEN*, 31 October 1953, p. 4, and 19 January 1954, p. 4.

11. E.S. Pankhurst, letter to *Daily Herald*, 12 December 1935, quoted in *NTEN*, 2 January 1954, p. 3.
12. R. Pankhurst, 'Sylvia and *New Times and Ethiopia News*', in Bullock and Pankhurst, *Sylvia Pankhurst*, p. 154.
13. Dugan and Lafore, *Days of Emperor and Clown*, p. 343.
14. R. Pankhurst, 'Sylvia and *New Times and Ethiopia News*', p. 158.
15. R. Pankhurst, *Counsel for Ethiopia*, p. 59.
16. See, for example, *NTEN*, 13 June 1936, p. 1.
17. *NTEN*, 4 July 1936, p. 6.
18. *NTEN*, 11 August 1945, p. 4.
19. *NTEN*, 1 August 1936, p. 4.
20. R. Pankhurst, 'Sylvia Pankhurst and the Spanish Civil War', text of paper given to the Sylvia Pankhurst Memorial Lecture 2004, at Wortley Hall, Sheffield on 17 September, p. 6.
21. D. Gluckstein, *A People's History of the Second World War: Resistance versus Empire* (London: Pluto Press, 2012), p. 17.
22. P. Piratin, *Our Flag Stays Red* (London: Lawrence and Wishart, 1978), p. 51.
23. Quoted in *NTEN*, 12 January 1937, p. 1.
24. Ibid.
25. E.S. Pankhurst, letter to Dr Martin, 26 September 1935, quoted in Pankhurst, *Counsel for Ethiopia*, p. 19.
26. *NTEN*, 'For Victory' supplement, 17 August 1940.
27. *NTEN*, 23 December 1939, 6 January 1940, and 13 January 1940, p. 3.
28. R. Pankhurst, *Sylvia Pankhurst: Artist and Crusader*, p. 184.
29. *NTEN*, 31 August 1940, p. 1.
30. R. Pankhurst, *Counsel for Ethiopia*, p. 45.
31. Ibid.
32. Ibid., p. 48.
33. Winslow, *Sylvia Pankhurst*, p. 189.
34. R. Pankhurst, *Counsel for Ethiopia*, p. 48.
35. Sir Henry Channon, 30 July 1935, quoted in Dugan and Lafore, *Days of Emperor and Clown*, p. 133.
36. R. Pankhurst, *The Ethiopians*, pp. 215–6.
37. K. Nkrumah, *The Autobiography of Kwame Nkrumah* (London: Panaf Books Limited, 1973), pp. 22–3.
38. R. Pankhurst, *Counsel for Ethiopia*, pp. 11–12.
39. Ibid., p. 80.
40. Ibid., p. 85.
41. R. Pankhurst, *Sylvia Pankhurst: Artist and Crusader*, p. 204.
42. *NTEN*, 15 June 1940, p. 2.
43. L. Sponza, 'The British government and the internment of Italians', in D. Cesarani and T. Kushner (eds), *The Internment of Aliens in Twentieth-Century Britain* (London: Frank Cass and Company Limited, 1993), p. 126.

44. *NTEN*, 22 June 1940, p. 2.
45. *NTEN*, 17 August 1940, p. 1.
46. *NTEN*, 24 August 1940, p. 1.
47. Richard and Rita Pankhurst, interview with author, 2 August 2012.
48. Sponza, *Divided Loyalties*, p. 102.
49. Ibid., pp. 100–1.
50. Ibid., p. 102.
51. See T. Colpi, 'The impact of the Second World War on the British Italian community', in Cesarani and Kushner, *The Internment of Aliens*, pp. 180–1.
52. *NTEN*, 22 June 1940, p. 4.
53. For a like view of the contradictions in the Second World War, see Gluckstein, *A People's History of the Second World War*.
54. R. Pankhurst, *Counsel for Ethiopia*, p. 98.
55. Quoted in ibid., p. 126.
56. Quoted in ibid., p. 133.
57. Quoted in ibid., p. 126.
58. Ibid., p. 103.
59. *NTEN*, 27 September 1941, p. 4.
60. R. Pankhurst, *Counsel for Ethiopia*, p. 141.
61. Quoted in ibid., p. 154.
62. *NTEN*, 10 January 1942, p. 1.
63. R. Pankhurst, *Counsel for Ethiopia*, p. 178.
64. Ibid., p. 209; S. Pankhurst, *British Policy in Eritrea and Northern Ethiopia* (Woodford Green: Sylvia Pankhurst, 1945), pp. 7–8.
65. Pankhurst, *British Policy in Eritrea and Northern Ethiopia*, p. 5.
66. Quoted in R. Pankhurst, *Counsel for Ethiopia*, p. 236.
67. Richard and Rita Pankhurst, interview with author, 2 August 2012.
68. Ibid.
69. R. Pankhurst, *Counsel for Ethiopia*, p. 221.
70. Quoted in ibid., p. 251.

CONCLUSION

1. M. Davis, *Sylvia Pankhurst: A Life in Radical Politics* (London: Pluto Press, 1999), p. 82.

Index

Latzko, Andreas 119
Laurie, Hannah 128
Laval, Pierre 131
League of Coloured People 133
League of Nations 121, 131–2, 138
Leeds Conference 1917 93, 102
'Left-Wing' Communism: An
    Infantile Disorder (pamphlet)
    107
Leigh, Mary 35–6, 56, 128
Lenin, Vladimir 89, 96–7, 101, 103,
    105–9, 117, 121
Levi, Paul 106
Liberal Association 5
Liberal government 1, 5–6, 20
Liberal Party 5, 6, 17, 19, 26–7, 51
    antiwar agitation 1870s 4
    rally 1906 1
    repressive policies against Ireland
        and India 5, 51
Liberalism 4
Liddington, Jill 17
Liebknecht, Karl 101
Life of Emmeline Pankhurst: The
    Suffragette Struggle for
    Women's Citizenship, The
    (1936) 128
Limehouse 62, 109
Liverpool 91, 99
Lloyd Garrison, William 9
Lloyd George, David 108
London campaigns 20–5
London Library 7
London Workers' Committee 95
Lopez, Leon (pseudonym) see
    McKay
Lusitania 72
Luxemburg, Rosa 101–2
Lvov, Prince 87–8
Lytton, Lady Constance 37

Macarthur, Mary 68, 81
Macdonald, Ramsay 93, 102
McKay, Claude 110–12
McKenna, Reginald 71

MacKereth, Gilbert 145
Maclean, John 78, 89
Maffey, Sir John 131
Makonnen, T.R. 140
Malatesta, Errico 116
Manchester 4–6, 10, 12–13, 19, 20
Manchester Equal Pay League 19
Mander, Geoffrey 144
Mann, Tom 21
Manningham Mills 10
March of the Women, The 28
marches see demonstrations
marriage 9, 60, 103, 123–4
Married Women's Property Act see
    Parliamentary Bills and Acts
Marsh, Charlotte 36
Martin, Selina 36
Marx, Eleanor 11
Marx, Karl 83, 136
Marxism 78–9, 148
matchwomen's strike see strikes
Maxton, James 120
Matteotti, Giacomo 120–1
Matteotti, Velia 127–8
Matters, Muriel 75
Mechanics Institutes 5
Middle East, divided up 121
Mile End 90–1
militancy
    industrial 69, 98, 149
    rent strike 80
    suffragettes 2, 16, 20–1, 24, 28,
        34–7, 44, 46–8, 52–3, 57, 64,
        93, 128–9, 148
    working-class 7, 19, 44, 149
Molotov, Vyacheslav 137
Montefiore, Dora 57, 104, 128
Moody, Dr Harold 133
Morel, E.D. 111
Morris, William 8, 83
Mosley, Oswald 135
mother and infant mortality rates
    125
Municipal School of Art 14
munitions workers 77–81, 85, 98